CW01653496

Manor Publications

Grimsby Evening Telegraph

MAXIMUM EFFORT

One Group at War

Patrick Otter

First published 1990

Manor Publications Ltd
10 Seymour Court
Manor Park
RUNCORN
Cheshire

in association with

Grimsby Evening Telegraph
80 Cleethorpe Road
GRIMSBY
South Humberside

ISBN 1-873428-01-4

*1. **previous page:** Flt Lt Clark and crew of 460 Squadron, RAF Binbrook.*
*2. **above:** 166 Squadron's Christmas dance at Kirmington, 1944.*

Contents

Introduction 7
Unquiet Skies at Elsham Wolds 8-18
Memories of another PM-M 19-20
The Light in the Sky 21-22
Secrets in the Mud at Ludford 23-36
The Wonders of Wickenby 37-49
A Bad Winter 50-53
Brothers 54
Kirmington's Proud Record 55-67
Johnny Boy 68
Defying All the Odds 69-77
A Pilot's Story 78-80
The Poles at Faldingworth 81-85
Beating the Chop at Binbrook 86-90
The Disaster at Mailley-Le-Camp 91-94
Lonely Dispersals 95-97
Touch Down on the Humber 98-100
A Lancaster's Story 101-111
The Other Battle 112
Village Inn at Binbrook 113
All Those Lovely Lads 114-115
Driving the Yellow Peril 116-117
The Lucky Ones 118
Dangerous Days – and Nights – at Waltham 119-120
Battle of the Buzz Bombs 121-122
Just Another Raid 123-124
The Bonds of Comradeship 125
A Rum Do 126
A Word of Thanks 127

3. ***above:*** *12 Squadron armourers at Wickenby included at least one pretty young Waaf in August 1944.*
4. ***below:*** *Cooks and messing staff, 626 Squadron, Wickenby, late 1944.*

Fifty Years On

NINETEEN-NINETY is a year of anniversaries: the Battle of France, Dunkirk, the Battle of Britain.

It is also the 50th anniversary of the reforming of 1 Group Bomber Command. It had been part of the pre-war Bomber Command structure, based at airfields in the South Midlands. But 1939 saw it disbanded and reformed as the Advanced Air Striking Force in France, a somewhat inappropriate title as events were to prove.

But after Dunkirk it was reformed at Hucknall in Nottinghamshire as Britain prepared to use the only means at its disposal to take the war to Germany — Bomber Command.

One of the first airfields the new 1 Group took over was Binbrook, high on the Lincolnshire Wolds, from where on a clear day you were able to see the Minster spires at Lincoln and York, the Stump at Boston and, of course, the Humber just beyond the fish docks at Grimsby.

Within a short time it was decided that the whole of 1 Group would be allocated to this area. Airfields were already under construction and soon they began to open: Elsham Wolds, Kirmington, Waltham, Wickenby, Ludford, Kelstern, Faldingworth, North Killingholme. There were airfields where the primary aim was training at Blyton, Sandtoft, Ingham, Sturgate and, just across the Yorkshire county boundary, at Lindholme.

1 Group, from a small beginning when it could muster just 12 aircraft, was to become one of the most powerful elements in Bomber Command, able to dispatch 300-plus Lancasters to anywhere in Europe, each aircraft carrying well in excess of the total bomb load of the entire group in late 1940.

This, then, is the second part of our look at 1 Group as we look in detail at two of the Base airfields, Elsham Wolds and Ludford, along with Faldingworth, Wickenby and Kirmington.

More importantly, we look at the men and women who served there. This, after all, is their story.

5. Ankle deep in daisies, Polish and British officers pictured at a service held at Faldingworth, the home of 300 Squadron.

6. 103's Honours Board tells its own story.

Unquiet Skies at Elsham Wolds

IT DOESN'T take a trained eye to determine the history of Elsham Wolds as you speed past on your way to or from the Humber Bridge.

For there, high on the last ramparts of the Lincolnshire Wolds, are the unmistakable remains of a Second World War bomber airfield. You can't make out the runways now, even though the A15 dual carriageway goes right across the point where the Wellingtons and Lancasters prepared to take off. But still highly visible are Elsham's two remaining T2 and distinctive J-Type hangars.

The old watch office, which was turned into a house after the war and was reputed to be haunted, has now been demolished. The hangars are storage warehouses, the dispersals have become lorry parks. Elsham is an industrial estate and was once briefly linked with a Japanese car manufacturer as a possible factory site.

It is all a far cry from the days of war when Elsham was among the busiest of all Bomber Command airfields. For part of the war it supported two Lancaster bomber squadrons and at various times was used by a Heavy Conversion Unit and acted as the relief landing ground for the training unit based at Blyton. In addition, Elsham was the headquarters of 1 Group's 13 Base, which included Kirmington and North Killingholme. It was to Elsham that the squadrons there sent their Lancasters for major servicing. Little wonder the skies around Elsham Wolds were rarely quiet.

How different it all was from 1940. Then, what was to become the airfield was farmland atop the Wolds, up the hill from the village of Elsham from which it took its name.

Three farmers worked the land which was chosen by the Air Ministry in 1940 as the site for a bomber airfield. When the rapid expansion of the RAF was given top priority, the men from the Ministry turned to the Great War for guidance on where to locate their new airfields. There had been a fighter airfield at Elsham (if the venerable FE2b could ever truly be called a fighter) in 1917 and it was a natural place for the Ministry surveyors to look in 1940.

7. S-Sugar of 103 Squadron, which was lost on a raid on Mannheim on September 5/6, 1943. All the crew survived and remarkably most escaped, either back to the UK or to Switzerland. Only the navigator became a PoW. They are (from the left): R.B. Cant, pilot, T. Thomas, navigator, E. Dickson, engineer, S. Hurton, wireless operator, B. Milburn, mid-upper gunner, T. Teare, bomb-aimer and B. Parkinson, rear gunner.

A young farmworker employed on one of the farms was asked to help in that survey. Ernest Hatcliffe, who had only just started to work and was anxious to do anything to help, was pleased to oblige. He held the poles while the surveyor aligned his theodolite. Ernest had little reason to imagine what an enormous difference that survey was to make to him and the lives of everyone living within a three mile radius.

It was a good site for a bomber airfield, just to the east of the landing ground once used by the wood-and-wire FEs, and within a few months the contractors had moved in to start laying the foundations for the runways, putting up the hangars and building the first of the accommodation sites, traces of which can still be found in the woods around Elsham.

Elsham Wolds had been designated as the home for 103 Squadron, one of the founder units of 1 Group when it was reformed in the summer of 1940 from the remnants of the Advanced Air Strike Force, which had just returned from the disasters which befell it in France.

103 Squadron had been operating from Newton in Nottinghamshire but the plans for Bomber Command meant that a move north was necessary; 1 Group had been earmarked for North Lincolnshire and 103 was to take the second airfield available, Binbrook being in use right from the beginning. So it was on July 11, 1941 that 103 moved in to Elsham Wolds, where it was to remain for the rest of the war, itself a record in 1 Group and perhaps in most of Bomber Command.

The squadron had been operating the Wellington 1C since the previous October and was to continue to fly this ubiquitous aircraft for exactly a year from Elsham Wolds. Work on the airfield was still going on when the squadron arrived but this was ever the case in wartime Britain. Ready or not, 103 was in action within three days of the move to Elsham, six aircraft bombing what they hoped was Bremen.

The news that Bomber Command had another operational airfield did not go unnoticed across the North Sea. In early August two German fighter bombers attacked Elsham, one being shot down within a few miles of the new bomber station.

8. PM-H of 103 Squadron, early summer 1943. The aircraft was badly damaged on August 23, 1943 after a raid on Berlin. She was later repaired and transferred to 576 Squadron and completed more than 50 ops before the war ended. Those on the picture include Doug Finlay, Jim Wivers (killed September 1943), Sandy Rowe, Harry Wheeler (killed at Elsham August 1943), Bill Gillespie, Sgt Steel, Ian Fletcher, John McFarlane and the MT driver, Peggy Forster.

The 103 Wimpeys were beginning to range far and wide. In September they bombed Turin in Northern Italy; by the end of the year the squadron was able to dispatch 17 Wellingtons in one raid.

There were losses, though nothing yet on the scale of those to come, and there was drama aplenty. On one raid a flare ignited inside a Wellington. Four of the crew baled out but the pilot, Sgt Spooner, and another member of the crew, Sgt Bray, brought the Wellington back to Elsham. The flare, it was later discovered, had fallen out of the aircraft before it could cause any mortal damage.

Ernest Hatcliffe, in the meantime, had married and he and his wife Gladys had moved into a farmworker's cottage actually on the airfield. They were issued with a pass to get to and from their own home, but they were not unduly worried. The RAF were good, if somewhat noisy, neighbours and there were few days went by when they didn't have some fresh-faced young sergeant or lonely Waaf knocking on their door.

At night the Hatcliffes would lie awake listening to the Wellingtons leaving and they would be up early the next day to see if any of the dispersals were empty.

May 1942 saw the first of the 1,000 bomber raids with Elsham sending 29 Wellingtons to Cologne. It was the start of a costly summer for 103 Squadron as night after night Wellingtons came back from raids with dead or wounded crew . . . or failed to come back at all.

In August 103 became the first squadron in 1 Group to convert to four-engined aircraft, not the Lancaster which was eventually to equip the entire group, but the Halifax II, the only squadron in the Group to fly this aircraft. It was not a particularly popular move. The Halifax was of the new generation of bombers but the Mk II was an aircraft with some nasty habits and lacked the performance of the Lancaster, which was just beginning to arrive in neighbouring 5 Group.

There was no Heavy Conversion Unit to train crews either. A 103 Squadron Conversion Flight was formed at Elsham and it was on this that new crews or those moving over from the Wellington were trained. It was in one of this Flight's Halifaxes that 12 young men perished that August when their aircraft crashed on the edge of the airfield.

The first Halifax operation from Elsham was against Dusseldorf and all returned safely. But 103 wasn't to keep its Halifaxes for long. It had already been decided that 1 Group should eventually become an all-Lancaster force and in November the first of the new Avro "heavies" arrived at Elsham, much to the delight of the men who had to fly them. The Lancaster I was a much superior aircraft to the early Halifaxes and by November 21 the conversion had been completed. 1 Group had its first Lancaster squadron.

Throughout that winter and spring, 103 played its part in the stepping up of the bombing campaign. On one night, May 23, 1943, the squadron sent 27 Lancasters to Duisburg to deliver 113 tons of bombs, a Bomber Command record at the time.

The Hatcliffes, in the meantime, had become an integral part of life at Elsham. Ernest himself was usually available to help supplement rations and his wife had become a surrogate mother for many of the young airmen. The kettle was always on and the station laundry was put to shame by her starched shirts and collars.

"I don't know how it all started," she said. "I suppose one of them came in for tea one day and asked if I would do his shirt for him. They wanted to look smart when they went home to their wives."

Eventually, Mrs Hatcliffe found she was washing 40 or 50 shirts at a time and there was a constant stream of visitors to their cottage door.

"Every so often someone would come round and ask for so-and-so's laundry because they were not coming back. That was when it really came home to us what those boys were doing."

The Hatcliffes, who now live in retirement in Barnetby, still have a photograph of "Red" Black and his crew. They brought their washing to Mrs Hatcliffe one afternoon before they were due to go on ops saying they would be back for it the following day. A few hours later their Lancaster was shot down and all seven members of the crew killed.

Another man with memories of the young aircrew at Elsham is Mr J.W. Curtis of Barrow Road, Barton-on-Humber. At the time he was working as a mechanic for Charles Atkinson, who ran the White Cross garage in the town during the war.

"A young pilot officer lived in the flat behind the garage with his young wife and I knew he was flying operationally from Elsham," said Mr Curtis. "He had a green 1936 Ford 8 with a clapped-out engine and it was very unreliable. I had replaced the engine of Birkitt's Ford 10 bread van and I put the engine which had come out of it into the airman's car. It was a gift from Mr Atkinson to the airman as a way of recognising the job he was doing. It was 200cc over size but it ran like a Rolls-Royce Merlin and I remember he drove it out of our yard to go to Elsham where he was due to fly.

"Scarcely a week went by when I realised he had not come back from that bombing raid. Three days later his wife left Barton for good."

9. ***above:*** *Butch Harris, the man who controlled the destiny of everyone in Bomber Command. He visited Elsham in September 1943.*
10. ***below:*** *The Equipment Section at Elsham Wolds.*

11. **above:** *The crew of L-London who delivered their washing to the Hatcliffes but never picked it up again.*
12. **below:** *The flight engineer of R-Roger of 576 Squadron relaxes in the afternoon sunshine at Elsham in 1944. The aircraft in the background is Mike-Squared, then on the strength of 576.*

It was officially frowned upon to have wives close to the airfield. But many a blind eye was turned to the practice.

Alex Temperley was a young pilot who was posted to 103 Squadron in September 1942 and arrived at Barnetby station with his wife one afternoon that month. They were determined to find somewhere to live in the village so that they could be together.

"We were lucky to meet a postman who suggested we try at a house called Stonecroft just outside the village and we lived there until I completed my tour at Elsham Wolds the following March," he said. (This house was later to become one of the Cheshire Homes set up by one of the most famous men Bomber Command produced during the war, Group Captain Leonard Cheshire VC.) "It was frowned upon by the authorities and not official, but with an understanding commanding officer we managed to do so.

"We became very attached to Miss Becky Moss, who had started life at Stonecroft as a governess to Mr Havercroft and was still looking after him although she was nearly 70."

Mr Temperley, who finally retired from the RAF as a squadron leader with a DFC, went on: "Their lives had been very sheltered and their way of living was so simple it was in welcoming contrast to my job of dropping bombs over Germany. I remember particularly one Sunday morning when she returned from church just as I was about to depart for the camp on my bicycle to prepare for a night raid. She just couldn't believe that we did such things on a Sunday; it was very wicked and shouldn't be done that day."

One of the most popular pilots on the squadron at this time was Flt Lt Florent Van Rolleghem, a Belgian pilot. In August 1943 he was awarded the Distinguished Flying Cross and the Belgian Croix de Guerre to go with his Distinguished Service Order. At a special parade, the medals were pinned on his chest by the AOC of 1 Group, Air Vice Marshal Edward Rice. Van Rolleghem later became a squadron leader with 103.

In September Elsham had a distinguished visitor when Air Chief Marshal Sir Arthur Harris, the C-in-C of Bomber Command, spent several hours at the airfield, meeting members of 103 Squadron, touring the site and watching the aircraft leave for an operation.

13. Air and ground crew of X-Xray of 103 Squadron. This was the aircraft of Flt Lt (later Sqdn Ldr) Van Rolleghem, a Belgian pilot who became one of the squadron's most decorated pilots. Among those on the photograph is John Lamming (third left, front), whose home was at Goxhill, only a few miles from Elsham. He was responsible that day for painting the Belgian and British flags on the aircraft together with the insignia marking X-Xray's 21st operation.

That November a second squadron was formed at Elsham. 103's C-Flight was detached and within a few days had formed the nucleus of 576 Squadron, which was to fly alongside its parent squadron for 11 months before moving to Fiskerton, which had just become a 1 Group airfield.

There was some friendly rivalry between the two squadrons during the time they flew together from Elsham and it was a friendship which was to blossom after the war. While many squadron associations were formed, a station association was formed by ex-103 and 576 Squadron members.

The two stations also shared aircraft. One was perhaps the most famous Lancaster of the lot, ED888, a Mk III which had first flown with 103 Squadron on a raid on Dortmund on May 4/5, 1943 and which was to retire in December 1944 after 140 operations.

The machine carried the code M2 and made her first 66 trips with 103 before transferring to 576 Squadron with which she was to fly 65 operational sorties. Then it was back to 103 for a further nine before this venerable Lancaster was finally retired with 974 operational hours to her credit. No fewer than 98 of her trips had been to Germany, the Lancaster taking part in 15 raids on Berlin alone. During her time at Elsham she also underwent a total of 19 engine changes. She later flew with a training unit before being broken up without ceremony at Tollington in 1947.

But one part of this famous Lancaster does remain. Her pilot for her last flight to Tollington was an ex-103 Squadron man who had flown her operationally and he rescued the bomb release cable from the Lancaster; it was later mounted and presented to the Elsham Wolds Association.

Interestingly, the aircraft is often referred to as "Mike-Squared", the name she was known by during her 576 Squadron days. But ex-103 men say they always knew her as Mother of Them All. The last surviving flying Lancaster, which is operated by the Battle of Britain Memorial Flight, is currently wearing the colours of this aircraft.

Elsham was by now a hive of activity. As many as 40 aircraft at a time were operating some nights and losses, inevitably, were high. On the night of February 19, 1944 three Lancasters were lost in a raid on Leipzig and two more destroyed in a runway collision. The Nuremburg raid cost

14. Bob Edie of Edinburgh, and air and ground crew of N-Nan of 103 Squadron showing 52 sortie symbols and some dashing nose art.

Elsham another three aircraft, two of them from 103, while no fewer than seven Lancasters from the Elsham squadrons were lost in the Mailly-le-Camp disaster in early May.

In that same raid, a 576 Squadron Lancaster was attacked by a night-fighter over the target but the pilot, Pilot Officer Reed, whose home was in Wellingborough, Northants, managed to evade the fighter. The Lancaster, however, caught fire, a large hole was blown in the floor of the cockpit, electrical and navigational instruments were smashed, the rudders and elevators were damaged and the rear turret had almost been shot away, But remarkably Reed, with his flight engineer helping at the controls and bomb-aimer operating the rudder pedals, brought the crippled Lancaster back to Elsham.

Two nights later the new Base commander at Elsham Wolds, Air Commodore R. Ivelaw-Chapman, opted to fly as second pilot in a 576 Squadron Lancaster in a raid on an ammunition dump at Aubigne in Northern France. Just one aircraft was lost from the 52 1 Group Lancasters which carried out a brilliantly accurate raid. It was the aircraft containing Air Commodore Ivelaw-Chapman.

He had only recently taken up his new job at Elsham after a staff post in the course of which he had access to information on the coming invasion. There was great concern that if he was taken prisoner and handed over to the Gestapo the invasion could be compromised.

Ivelaw-Chapman, a vastly experienced airman already with a Distinguished Flying Cross and an Air Force Cross, was indeed taken prisoner. But the Germans never realised the importance of their prisoner and he saw out the war in a PoW camp. His place as Base commander was taken by Air Commodore F.R.D. Swain, once the holder of the world altitude record.

That the invasion secrets had not been disclosed was evident to the Elsham squadrons when they were among the very first Allied units to go into action on D-Day itself, bombing batteries overlooking the landing beaches in Normandy.

That June both Elsham squadrons were to drop more than 1,000 tons of bombs as the campaign against French targets reached a new peak of ferocity. It was now, as the bombers flew increasingly in daylight or in the dusk of the long, double-summertime evenings, that people in North Lincolnshire probably realised for the first time the full extent of the Bomber Command presence in their area. Hundreds of aircraft could be seen rising from the airfields as they set off to bomb railway junctions, ammunition dumps and V-bomb sites. In one attack alone, the Elsham squadrons dispatched 42 Lancasters which, between them, could carry as great a tonnage of bombs as an entire Bomber Command raid earlier in the war.

But German targets in particular were still heavily defended and Elsham lost eight Lancasters in one night attack in July on Stuttgart, a 20 per cent loss rate in just one raid. Several more limped

15. The air and ground crew and R-Roger of 576 Squadron. Note the splendid nose art on this B Flight aircraft.

back to Elsham bearing the scars of flak and night-fighter damage.

In the same raid 103 Squadron exacted some revenge when two of its Lancasters were each attacked by a pair of fighters and claimed all four as shot down.

Early in October 103 and 576 flew 86 sorties in less than 24 hours against Duisburg, dropping a colossal 1,277 tons of bombs in the process, an average of almost 15 tons of bombs per aircraft. Examining the records of other squadrons for this attack, this appeared to be about the 1 Group norm that day.

The availability of more airfields led to the decision to move 576 and this was completed at the end of the month, the squadron operating from this airfield close to Lincoln for the remainder of the war.

103 had long prided itself on the ability of its ground crews which, it maintained with some justification, were among the best in 1 Group and probably the whole of Bomber Command. They were certainly put to the test early in 1945 when two Lancasters collided while taxiing. The tail section of one aircraft was wrecked while the main spar of the second was twisted. Within just 46 hours the two aircraft had been cut in half and the "good bits" welded together to form a hybrid Lancaster which flew operationally the same night, though the records do not make clear whether as K-King or B-Baker, the two aircraft which had collided.

It was back to two squadrons at Elsham from April 1 when 100 moved in from Waltham, and both took part in the final raid of the war on Berchtesgarten on April 25.

Then the Elsham Lancasters began mercy flights, dropping food supplies to the Dutch and ferrying home PoWs.

There was no dramatic end for Elsham itself. Just a gradual wind-down. The Lancasters moved out in the autumn to be replaced by Albemarles and later Halifax glider tugs. But the airfield itself was showing distinct signs of the heavy wartime use and eventually flying ended altogether.

"It was strange when it was over," said Mrs Hatcliffe. "It all seemed to happen very gradually until one day they weren't there anymore."

The Hatcliffes and all the other Lincolnshire folk whose lives were centred around Elsham Wolds were left with the crumbling remains of a wartime airfield and their memories of the bright-eyed young men who had gone to war just across the potato field.

16. Flying control at Elsham. This became a house after the war and was reputed to be haunted.

17. One of Elsham's most famous photographs, the bestowing of a bar to the DFC on M-Squared, then on the strength of 576 Squadron.

Memories of another PM-M

MIKE-SQUARED may have been Elsham's most famous Lancaster, but Tommy Quinlan can tell you a story or two about the original PM-M of 103 Squadron, at least the bit of it that he flew in.

The Lancaster, NF913, had been wrecked in a crash landing at Elsham in 1943 and it was later cut in half and joined to the rear of PM-H, going on to fly almost 50 operational sorties before being lost in March 1945 on a raid on Dessau.

It was the aircraft allocated to Welsh gunner Tommy Quinlan, who was to marry a local girl and now lives in Scunthorpe, and his crew when they flew their first op with 103 on the night of August 25/26, 1944 when 1 Group Lancasters hit the Opel factory at Russelheim.

Thirty-six aircraft left Elsham, 18 from each of the squadrons. Ironically, the only one to turn back was 576's Mike-Squared. It had a faulty rear turret.

In many ways it was a copy-book attack, with the Pathfinders marking the target accurately and much of the factory being damaged in a raid which lasted just 10 minutes.

It was also a night when the night-fighters were active, very active as far as the new crew from Elsham was concerned. The pilot, Pilot Officer "Selmo" Vernieuwe, a Belgian, later reported eight encounters with fighters, three of which turned into full blooded combats.

The station narrative of operations described what happened next: "As he (P/O Vernieuwe) was approaching the target, a Me410 was dealt with by the mid-upper gunner, Sgt Relf, who sent it down in flames into cloud and claims it probably destroyed. On the homeward route a FW190 attacked and it was sent down in flames by the rear gunner (Sgt Quinlan), who saw it crash and explode on the ground and therefore claims it destroyed. A later engagement with an unidentified aircraft proved inconclusive. A good start for this crew's first operational trip."

What the narrative didn't report was that during one of the combats, the Lancaster plunged from 18,000 to 2,000 feet during which "a few rivets popped".

18. The original PM-M and the crew which shot down two fighters on their first operation, pictured at Elsham in September 1944. They are (standing, from the left): Sgt Quinlan, rear gunner, P/O Othen, navigator, F/O Jones, wireless operator, F/O Vernieuwe, pilot, and F/O Seaton, bomb-aimer; (seated) Sgt Relf, mid-upper gunner, and Sgt Wells, engineer.

It was during this same raid that a second 103 Lancaster, PM-T, flown by Flying Officer Ryerse, shot down a Ju88 and claimed as damaged a Me110.

The following night, with rivets replaced, PM-M and crew were back on operations again, this time raiding Kiel. There were no combats this time but the crew did spot a dinghy in the North Sea believed to contain the crew of a missing bomber. A message was later received from Group HQ at Bawtry Hall saying the sighting helped the ASR to locate the dinghy, which contained the seven members of a Canadian crew who had ditched after a raid on Hamburg.

A few days later PM-M was sporting 13 bomb symbols, two swastikas and a miniature dinghy painted on the nose.

P/O Vernieuwe and his crew later went on to fly Elsham's more famous "M" and brought it back from the raid on the Wanne-Eickel refinery in November with serious flak damage. It was soon after that that Elsham's veteran retired.

There were a few more hairy trips for P/O Vernieuwe's crew before they completed their tour in January 1945, including one when they just made it into the emergency airfield at Woodbridge in Suffolk with two engines out of action.

19. F/O Vernieuwe at the controls of PM-M. Note the two swastikas and dinghy symbol on the nose.

The Light in the Sky

ONE EX-PILOT with very fond memories of his days at Elsham is Mike Stedman, who flew with 576 during the summer of 1944.

His log book shows 32 operations with the squadron but a number of them were actually flown from Binbrook where, for a three-month period, his crew was attached to the Binbrook Special Duties Flight.

This was a special hybrid Flight which had been set up in the late spring as a move to form a 1 Group "pathfinder" unit. Each squadron in the Group supplied one crew and they operated as a special, distinct unit at Binbrook.

They practised low flying, the pilots wearing blacked-out goggles and the bomb-aimer and the flight engineer guiding the pilot around any obstacles in their way.

The Flight did provide marking for a number of 1 Group attacks but Mike Stedman recalls that most of the operations he flew from Binbrook were simply as part of Main Force attacks.

Elsham itself he remembers as a happy station. It was a short bike ride down to Barnetby station to catch the train into Scunthorpe where they would meet with other crews at the Oswald or visit a girl friend at the YM.

He also recalls a trip up the hill to the camp from the Waafery in Barnetby in the wing commander's car after a dance.

20. A good turn-out for I-Item of of 576 Squadron taking off for its first sortie, to Orleans on July 4, 1944. At the controls was Mike Stedman who went on to complete a full tour with the squadron. This aircraft was to survive the war, completing its 100th trip just nine months later on a Manna food drop over Holland.

"We had a full load and my bomb-aimer was standing in the boot pretending to throw out 'window' to confuse the defences when someone shouted: 'Fighter, fighter, corkscrew starboard!'. The cars swerved and pitched my luckless bomb-aimer out of the boot and over a nearby hedge. Happy days!"

Throughout his flying career he always felt the main enemy of a wartime bomber pilot was fog, something which was reinforced by the events of the night of October 27, 1943.

He was then at 83 OTU at Peplow, flying a Wellington X on circuits and bumps, when the fog suddenly closed in. They were diverted to Little Rissington but, as they were on the approach, they hit an unseen object which broke off a wing tip.

"We climbed through the fog only to find our other diversion airfield was closed so we transmitted a May-Day and waited for a friendly night-fighter to guide us to a fog-free airfield.

"A bright white light appeared on the port side, flying on an easterly course at about 3,000 feet. I formated on the light but by now our fuel was beginning to get low as we had been airborne for four hours.

"Then we passed over an illuminated airfield, lost height and joined the circuit when the starboard engine packed up on the down-wind leg. As we feathered it, the starboard engine misfired so I selected wheels up and belly landed on the grass."

They had landed at Binbrook and they just got down as the fog closed in there, too. It was so thick that the transport driver sent out to bring them in had great difficulty in finding their Wellington.

The station CO at Binbrook, who Mike Stedman was to see a lot of in his operational days, Group Captain Hughie Edwards VC, made a point of congratulating the crew on a fine effort. But there was less praise back at Peplow. His log book was endorsed: "Carelessness. Taking off for flying duties in Wellington without essential navigational maps and instruments." It appears his navigator had not taken his bag of maps and instruments with him for what was only supposed to be an evening's sessions of circuits and bumps.

One thing about that night which still puzzles Mike Stedman is that try as he may, he has never been able to find any record of a night-fighter intercepting a May-Day call that night!

21. M-Mother and friends, 103 Squadron, March 1944. With the RAF's most famous Lancaster are (from the left): Arthur Richardson DFC, navigator Ron Walker DFC, wireless operator Jack Spark DFM, Bob Thomas (who was killed that night in a raid on Berlin) and the pilot, Fred Brownines DFC.

Secrets in the Mud at Ludford

"A JOKE in very bad taste played by the Air Ministry at our expense." That was how the commander of RAF Ludford Magna described the station in his Christmas message to the unfortunate airmen and women who found themselves posted there in the winter of 1944, a full 18 months after it had opened.

Ludford Magna came to be regarded as the worst possible posting in 1 Group — for aircrew because of the perils on operations there, for everyone else because of the appalling conditions which didn't improve until the last few months of the war.

The official records show it took Air Ministry contractors Wimpeys eleven months to build RAF Ludford Magna. Most of that time was spent on the runways and the dispersals on a site high on an undulating section of the Lincolnshire Wolds. Rumour, and there is nothing stronger to go on, suggests the accommodation sites were put up in just 30 days. And it showed.

Some ground crew spent the first few months at Ludford sleeping on the cinema floor. The less fortunate ones had tents.

It was muddy even before the RAF moved in. The passage of 1,000 men, their lorries, bowsers, generators and eventually their aircraft churned the airfield into a quagmire in no time at all.

Rainwater would seep into one end of a Nissen hut and emerge from the other. Duckboards were laid but rapidly disappeared. For all the world it looked like Flanders 26 years earlier.

Yet out of all this emerged a bomber squadron which was chosen for a very special task and which was to acquit itself magnificently during the two remaining years of war.

101 had been selected by Bomber Command as its first electronic counter measures squadron. The reason for the selection of this particular squadron is not clear, but it probably had something to do with the fact that Group Captain Bobby Blucke was the first station commander. He was a man who had pioneered the use of radar in aircraft and, apart from being a first class airman, was an enthusiastic supporter of anything which might improve the chances of the bomber crews.

Bomber Command had up its sleeve a device code-named ABC (which inevitably became known as Air-Borne Cigar) which was simply a listening and transmitting post within a Lancaster bomber aimed at disrupting night-fighter operations.

The Luftwaffe had developed a very sophisticated control system for their fighters, ground controllers using the radar network to identify bombers and then vector the night-fighters on to them, the fighters then relying on either visual sighting or their own air-to-air radar to make the final contact.

ABC involved a German-speaking operator becoming the eighth member of the Lancaster's crew. His job was to scan the frequencies looking for the fighter controllers and then, once he had identified their channels, to jam them. His job was not, as has been suggested in some reports on ABC, to broadcast false messages, but simply to disrupt the transmissions.

22. 101 Squadron, spring 1945. When Roy Chadwick designed the Lancaster and worked out the wing loading, he could hardly have had a scene like this in his mind!

To be effective, it was necessary that the ABC aircraft should be spread throughout the bomber stream. And it also meant that aircraft from 101 had to fly on every major raid, something which contributed largely to their very heavy losses while flying from Ludford. If, for instance, just 5 Group aircraft were operating, 101 would provide probably five or six Lancasters to accompany them.

The ABC Lancasters would be stationed in pairs at regular intervals in the bomber stream so that if one was shot down that section of the stream would still be covered.

It was a highly secret operation. When *Illustrated* magazine sent its photographers to Ludford in January 1944 to prepare material to show what life was like on a front-line RAF station, all photographs of aircraft were actually taken at Wickenby. The ABC Lancasters had two large dorsal aerials and a third mounted under the cockpit and the censor was quick to erase any he saw in the few photographs of Ludford which came his way. Many other unofficial ones were taken and some are reproduced here.

ABC remained with 101 and 1 Group throughout the war in spite of the creation of 100 Group, which specialised in radio and electronic counter measures.

The first ABC-equipped Lancaster flew with 101 Squadron in a raid on Stuttgart on October 7, 1943. This, and the second ABC Lancaster delivered to the squadron, was quickly lost, leading to the mistaken belief that somehow the German radar could lock onto ABC transmissions. And when two more aircraft arrived some crews were reluctant to fly them. But fly they must and the aircraft were taken by the commanders of A and B Flights and both returned safely. By the end of November the squadron had its full allocation of ABC aircraft, operating these alongside some "normal" Lancasters.

The special operator was located in the aircraft just forward of the main spar. Bomber Command combed its squadrons for German-speakers, or rather German-listeners, and then attached the special operators to crews at Ludford.

But back to the mud . . .

It was in June 1942 when the Air Ministry surveyors chose a site just south of Ludford Magna, on the Louth-Market Rasen road, for one of its new bomber airfields. It was a familiar A-pattern layout with dispersed sites in and around Ludford Magna itself. It opened on June 15, 1943 when 101 Squadron arrived from Holme-on-Spalding Moor in their Lancasters.

101 brought with them a history which stretched back to the Royal Flying Corps days and a motto, Mens Agitat Molem (Mind Over Matter), which seemed wholly appropriate when they caught their first glimpse of Ludford. There was hardly a blade of grass to be seen. From the air it looked like a huge scar on the landscape with runways and a few buildings dotted around.

Arthur Miles was an electrician who had been with 101 for the past 15 months when he arrived at Ludford. "We were told there was no accommodation for us and we were given 'biscuit' mattresses and had to sleep on the floor of the cinema," he said. "It was six months before we were to get proper accommodation."

23. MacNamara's Band of 101 undergoing maintenance at Ludford.

It was quickly dubbed Mudford Magna by the men who, even that summer, had to battle through ankle-deep mud to get to messes or dispersals. Gum boots were issued. Some areas were so bad that an airman could be placed on a charge for venturing into certain very muddy parts. Paths were laid and woe betide anyone who strayed off them.

Herbert Harrison, who flew as a flight engineer with 101 in the later stages of the war, recalls that conditions were still very bad when he arrived there. "It was a quagmire," he said. "Before I went I was warned the most important thing at Ludford was a good pair of gum boots. When I arrived I found out why! There was no doubt it was a grim place. You even needed to put your gum boots on to go to the toilet in the night."

It wasn't all mud, though. This area of the Lincolnshire Wolds can be very attractive when it is not raining and the airmen were quick to discover some of the local beauty spots, including Tealby (described by one as "the most beautiful village I have seen") and Benniworth Haven, a tree-shrouded fishing pond which Lord Heneage allowed Ludford personnel to use as a swimming pool.

But despite the problems on the ground, the war in the air had to go on. In that summer and early autumn of 1943 101 flew as part of the Main Force on all the big raids, including Hamburg and Peenemunde.

Then came the advent of ABC. The new role did not diminish 101's primary task of dropping bombs on enemy targets. Normal bomb loads were carried less the weight of the ABC equipment and the extra crew member.

Indeed John Wickman, who served as a fitter-armourer at Ludford, remembers the day a convoy of bombs arrived and it stretched right round the airfield. The bomb dumps were along Caistor High Street, part of which was closed off to traffic, and there were certainly no special concessions to 101 Squadron.

It was not long after the complete switch to ABC Lancasters that an aircraft from Ludford crashed in the grounds of Scallows Hall, four miles from the airfield. The Lancaster, which was on a night-flying exercise, came in low and clipped the top of the trees which surrounded Binbrook Hall. It went out of control and came down half a mile away in the grounds of Scallows Hall. The Hall was occupied at the time by a Mrs Burkinshaw, whose brother, Squire William Wright, lived in nearby Wold Newton. He was called to the Hall that night by his groom and was relieved to find his sister and her staff at the Hall had escaped although the crew of the Lancaster had all died. Squire Wright was convinced the pilot had sacrificed his own life by hauling the stricken aircraft clear of the Hall and he was so grateful that he erected a substantial memorial in Scallows Wood to the pilot and the crew.

Wing Commander Robert Alexander, who was CO of 101 Squadron from January to June 1944, was at Ludford during the squadron's darkest days, when they lost six aircraft on the Nuremburg raid and five over Mailly-le-Camp, but during that time remembers only one pilot going LMF — lacking moral fibre.

"Everyone had their private grief, I suppose. But we had to carry on. We all realised there was a

24. The day after Schweinfurt. SR-C of 101 Squadron pictured after a crash landing. Note the ABC aerials.

job to do and there was a degree of fatalism among the crews. They knew the odds were against them but they still carried on," he said.

One great monument for morale at Ludford was Group Captain and later Air Commodore Blucke, one of the finest airmen and one of the finest men Wing Commander Alexander came across during his own distinguished wartime career.

He was a man everyone at Ludford looked upon with the greatest respect and admiration. Blucke made it an unwritten rule that whenever the squadron lost three or more aircraft he personally would fly as a captain on the next operation. No station could have asked for a finer leader.

Wing Commander Alexander himself flew on 12 operations during the six months he was in charge of CO. Whenever a pilot went sick he would take his crew on operations and flew three times to Berlin and to Schweinfurt and Stuttgart, as well as making "absolutely certain" he flew operationally on D-Day.

Ludford was right at the centre of the great circle of airfields in Lincolnshire and the abiding memory of villagers in the area is of seeing (or hearing on the dark nights) a great mass of circling Lancasters as they all sought to gain height before forming their stream and heading out across Mablethorpe or down to Norfolk on the first leg of their journey.

They were puzzled one foggy night when they saw the sky around Ludford lit by what looked like a huge blaze. They were even more puzzled when they heard aircraft landing. It was the first night Ludford's new FIDO system had been brought into operation. It was one of only 15 airfields in the country to be equipped with the special fog dispersal equipment, which consisted of burning up to 60,000 thousand gallons of fuel in special troughs at the side of the runway. The heat produced lifted the fog, giving aircraft the opportunity to land in what would otherwise have been been impossible conditions. But FIDO did have its drawbacks. The flames also produced considerable turbulence over the airfields and pilots found the upward draught from the fires so intense their aircraft were reluctant to land. A Lancaster had almost to be forced down on the runway.

Some of the first crews who tried it found the experience so alarming they chose to head for diversion airfields. But Group Captain Blucke did what he could to soothe the nerves of those pilots

25. The control tower at Ludford Magna, 1945. The white paint and the flower tubs would suggest this was taken during the first summer of peace in Europe.

who were unsure, even going as far as taking off in the station's communications aircraft, an Airspeed Oxford, to show them how to do it.

FIDO was also fitted at two other North Lincolnshire airfields, Sturgate and Fiskerton, and until the advent of blind landing aids it was the only way of getting aircraft down in very bad conditions. Some 101 aircrew claimed that during trials they were able to see their airfield while over the Channel!

Ludford was a regular target for German intruders. Indeed, after the war a comprehensive plan of the airfield was found amongst captured Luftwaffe documents. The plan accurately showed the layout of the runways, dispersals and the technical sites. And the map was dated May 1943, a month before the airfield actually opened. It would be interesting to learn how the Germans came by that information.

In October 1943 Wickenby officially became a satellite of Ludford and two months later Ludford became the headquarters of 14 Base, which also took in Faldingworth. All the major aircraft maintenance for the Base was to be centred on Ludford and three additional hangars were built and 14 Base Major Servicing Units formed.

That was a particularly cruel winter for those at Ludford. After the mud of the previous autumn came the frosts, the winds and the snow of a very pernicious winter. Often everyone (including aircrew) would be out on snow clearing operations. There were very few occasions when 1 Group squadrons were not able to operate because of snow principally because of the Herculean task which was often undertaken daily to clear the snow from the runways. On one occasion the main runway was partly cleared and the Lancasters took off empty, flew to Wickenby, were bombed up and refuelled and flew back to Ludford, which had now been fully cleared, ready for that night's operations.

101 was always in the forefront of innovations within 1 Group and it is almost certain to have been the first squadron fitted with the new Rose rear turret, which finally gave Lancasters heavier armament than the .303 Brownings. Certainly an early example of the turret was air tested there in March 1944.

It was in the same month that 101 suffered its most terrible night of the war. On March 30 Bomber Command raided Nuremburg. Bad planning, a great deal of good fortune on the part of the

26. A 101 Squadron Lancaster unloading a cookie and incendiaries over Duisburg in a daylight raid in October 1944. Copies of this photograph were sold to ground crew at Ludford a few months later.

Luftwaffe night-fighter force plus a change in the weather and the winds led to the 795 aircraft being subjected to the most intensive opposition so far offered. The bomber stream was badly mauled along almost its entire length and that probably accounted for why 101 Squadron had six aircraft shot down and another lost in a crash in England. Its aircraft were strung out along the stream and 47 of the men on board died.

The loss of seven aircraft out of 26 sent speaks for itself. John Wickman remembers the following day on the airfield. "There were a lot of empty dispersals. Almost a third of the squadron had gone overnight and I can still picture all those weeping Waafs around Ludford that morning. But new aircraft and replacement crews arrived and within a day or two it was as though nothing had happened," he said. Such was life and death on a bomber station.

Five weeks later 101 suffered badly again when five aircraft were lost in the attack on Mailly-le-Camp. But there was a miraculous (and that is not too strong a word) escape for one of the squadron's rear gunners that night. Sgt Jack Worsford's aircraft was attacked by a night-fighter and the tail section, complete with his turret, broke away from the main fuselage with Worsford still trapped inside it. It fell from approximately 5,000 feet like a sycamore seed before it struck a set of electricity cables and, according to one member of his squadron, simply "bounced" off them. Sgt Worsford climbed out of the wreckage of his turret dazed but unhurt. He is still an active member of the 101 Squadron Association and has returned to the Mailly-le-Camp area where he has met the French family who hid him before he was eventually captured.

By now Bomber Command was switching its targets to Northern France to help pave the way for the invasion and it had a special role to play on D-Day as one of the squadrons which dropped window, the thin aluminium-coated strips which confused German radar, to help mask the approach of the invasion fleet to the Normandy beaches. They also carried out pin-point attacks in front of stalled American troops fighting their way on to the Cherbourg peninsular and took part in all the major attacks which aided the Allied advance that summer.

Then it was back to Germany that autumn and to the familiar pattern. ABC Lancasters went with all the major raids that autumn and winter and into the following spring.

It was a 101 Squadron gunner who claimed to have shot down the first jet fighter claimed by Bomber Command. But Sgt Sturrock in L-London may have fired at a rocket projectile which then exploded during an attack on Bochum.

101 remained at Ludford through the first summer of peace and moved out finally in October 1945. Fittingly, it was raining heavily at the time.

27. Formal group at Ludford in 1944. Note the airman eighth from the left on the back row holding the ABC aerial.

28. Sidney Smith of Louth pictured in 1984 at the Scallows Wood memorial to a 101 Squadron aircraft which crashed at this spot in December 1943.

29. ***left:*** *J-Joe pictured at Ludford in late 1943 by which time it was already a veteran. It was one of the Lancasters 101 brought with them from Holme-on-Spalding Moor.*

30. ***right:*** *Ludford-on-the-Mud, early spring 1943. On the extreme right is the rear gunner, Bob Wood, a Canadian who was to spend the final few months of the war with 101. The photograph comes from Harry Merrikin, formerly of Louth, Lincs, who now lives in Ontario.*

31. ***left:*** *Group Captain Blucke pictured at a Christmas party at Ludford in 1943.*

32. **right:** *Water carrying duties at Ludford. In the background are the CTO's office, stores and workshops.*

33. **above:** *Eyes in the sky. The aerial cameras carried in the Lancasters pictured in the photographic workshop at Ludford.*

34. **right:** *101 Squadron prided itself on the artwork on its aircraft. This was T-Tommy and groundcrew, pictured after her 14th trip.*

35. ***left:*** *The ops room at Ludford. In the centre on the telephone is the Base commander, Group Captain Blucke.*

36 & 37. ***right and below:*** *101's two veterans, H-Harry and S-Sugar. There was an unofficial race between these aircraft to become 101's top scorer. S-Sugar, pictured here being bombed up, was lost over Bremen in March 1945 on her 125th op. Harry made it to 121, by which time the Lanc had been awarded an honorary "Naafi gong".*

38. ***right:*** *Len Brooks pictured in the turret of his 101 Squadron Lancaster.*

39. ***below:*** *Coffee, rum and a chat with the padre after ops at Ludford, 1944.*

40. ***left:*** *Clearing the snow at Ludford, February 1944.*

41. ***middle:*** *A non-ABC Lancaster from 101 Squadron, R-Roger, pictured on a daylight raid over France in the summer of 1944.*

42. ***below:*** *A strange glow in the sky . . . Ludford's FIDO fog dispersal system in action.*

43. ***above:*** *There was quite a story behind the name painted on the side of this 103 Squadron Lancaster, which operated from Wickenby during 1944.*
It was on the strength of 12 Squadron and was allocated to a crew who had already survived a ditching in the North Sea on their 13th operation.
It came after their Lancaster had been attacked in a raid and they were picked up and returned to the squadron where they were issued with a new Lancaster, which had been allocated the code W when it arrived at Wickenby.
"It seemed a natural name to give it after our ditching," said mid-upper gunner Bryan Cooksley, who now lives in Eastbourne. "Who said 13 was unlucky?"
Six of the Wet Willie's flying crew appear on this picture together with two members of the ground crew. They include Sgt Ken Allum, navigator, Sgt Doug Snape, bomb-aimer, Flt Lt Howard Thomas, pilot, Sgt Allan Pollard, engineer, Sgt Cookson and Sgt Jock Gormley, rear gunner. Missing from the picture is Sgt Alf Silletoe, wireless operator.

44. Emily Warwick: she had never heard of Wickenby.

The Wonders of Wickenby

EMILY WARWICK remembers the day she was posted to RAF Wickenby. She had never heard of the place and was surprised to learn it was only 25 miles from her home in Grimsby.

Wickenby was, in fact, the archetypal wartime Lincolnshire RAF station: miles from anywhere, covered in mud, tin huts and bitterly cold in the winter.

Yet for exactly two years it operated at a peak of efficiency as a 1 Group bomber station, first supporting one, and later two, squadrons of Lancaster bombers. And many of the several thousand young men and women who served there between September 1942 and the day almost three years later when the war came to an end remember it as a friendly, well-run station.

Ivor Burgess was an RAF regular, a wireless fitter whose job took him to most of the 1 Group stations. He regarded Wickenby as one of the best and gave much of the credit to the station commander, Group Captain Basil Crummy, who was to spend most of those two years at Wickenby before he became CO at Sandtoft.

"The quality of a particular station was usually down to the station commander. Some were very good, others were lousy," said Mr Burgess. "Group Captain Crummy at Wickenby was one of the best I ever came across. He was a gentleman of the old type and treated everyone around him like gentlemen."

He said Wickenby was particularly fortunate during his time there to have Wing Commander Craven as CO of 12 Squadron. "Together they made it a very good station."

Group Captain Crummy was appointed CO in May 1943 by which time Wickenby had already been an operational station for almost nine months. It had opened in September 1942 as a satellite of RAF Binbrook and it was to Wickenby that 12 Squadron and its Wellingtons moved when Binbrook was closed operationally for the construction of hardened runways. 12 was one of the original 1 Group squadrons and had moved into Binbrook in June 1940 with its Fairey Battles. It had operated Wellingtons operationally from the airfield atop the Wolds for almost 18 months before its move to the new airfield on the flat agricultural plain between Market Rasen and Wragby.

John Wilkin was a Wellington navigator who was posted to 12 along with its crew while the squadron was still operating from Binbrook. By the time they arrived they found the squadron had moved to Wickenby and he and his crew were "loaned" to 101 Squadron, then at Holme-on-Spalding Moor in East Yorkshire. They did three trips with 101 before being told they were needed back at 12 Squadron which had suffered heavy casualties on a series of raids on Germany.

45. The local to the Wickenby squadrons, the White Hart at Lissington. Wickenby reunions are still held there.

"When we arrived the place seemed empty apart from tearful Waafs. All the crews that were left had been sent on leave and we were sent with them."

Mr Wilkin went on to do 12 operations with the squadron before joining a Pathfinder squadron at Warboys. But he still looks back on his period at Wickenby as one of the toughest he spent with Bomber Command.

That November 12 became the first squadron in 1 Group to begin converting to the new Lancaster, flying them for the first time against German targets on January 12, 1943 in a raid on Essen.

By April 12 Squadron had 27 Lancasters on strength and formed a third flight on May 14. It was now one of the most powerful squadrons in the whole of Bomber Command. The squadron's Wellingtons were transferred to 199 Squadron which was forming at Blyton and the last of these crashed on take-off from Wickenby after an engine failure on March 18.

The station was expanding rapidly and in mid-May 1943 the new No 6 accommodation site opened at Fulnetby, a couple of miles from the airfield. But, as the station records pointed out, it was far from complete, and there was no water or electricity. The records reported: "It is only suitable for sleeping at the moment."

Most of the accommodation was on dispersed sites and was rudimentary in the extreme. "Bloody awful" is how one airman remembers it. Flight engineer Geoff Robinson recalls the bleakness of the place, particularly during the winter he served there. There was never enough coal to go around for the stoves in the huts and he remembers returning from bombing raids to go on coal raids to try to find enough fuel to get reasonably warm.

Conditions weren't much different in the Waafs. Their accommodation was a 10-minute bike ride away on the far side of Wickenby village. Emily Warwick, too, remembers the grim winters. "We had icicles hanging from the roof and our towels would freeze onto the backs of the chairs we left them on overnight. We would put a bucket of snow on the stove and heat it up and 10 of us would use it for washing and then to fill our hot water bottles."

But delivering bombs was what Wickenby was all about. When Group Captain Crummy moved in from RAF Breighton 12 Squadron was in the midst of a period of heavy attacks on Germany.

46. Eric Parker and crew, 626 Squadron, Wickenby, 1944.

Three aircraft had been lost in the previous week in raids on Duisburg and Bochum and another was to be lost three nights later over Dortmund when 12 Squadron provided 21 aircraft for a Main Force raid. Almost every raid cost 12 Squadron a crew. Sgt Steel failed to return from Dusseldorf, Flying Officer Mounsey from Dortmund, Flt Lt Goudge from Wuppertal. One air gunner died when he failed to plug in his oxygen supply correctly and spent 52 minutes at a height between 25,000 and 20,000 feet on a journey back from the Ruhr.

But some crews had luck running their way. Sgt Scott and his crew had been on a gardening trip — minelaying — in their Lancaster in the Bay of Biscay when they were forced to ditch after suffering flak damage. They were to spend several very uncomfortable hours in a dinghy before being picked up by a minesweeper and landed at Dover. After a spell in hospital they were all sent on 10 days' leave.

Wickenby was able to give the people of Market Rasen an insight into what they were doing during Wings for Victory week when they put on a display in the Corn Exchange and 150 airmen marched through the town, followed by a tractor towing a 4,000lb "cookie".

The station's worst night of the war so far came on June 11/12 when 12 Squadron lost five Lancasters on a raid on Dusseldorf. Almost 800 aircraft devastated a large area of the city that night at a cost of 38 aircraft.

The Ruhr was proving a killing ground for Wickenby Lancasters that summer. Oberhausen, Cologne, Bochum, Krefeld, Mulheim, Wuppertal, Gelsenkirchen, all followed in quick succession, and most claimed Wickenby crews. At the end of the month the station medical officer reported five cases of lack of confidence amongst aircrews. Little wonder after a month which had seen almost half the squadron strength lost on operations or crashed on exercises.

Five more aircraft were lost in July as attacks on the Ruhr continued. 12 Squadron played its part in the devastation of Hamburg, flying almost 100 sorties in the attacks which almost obliterated Germany's second city. The raids cost the squadron two aircraft plus a badly shaken third when Sgt Jack Currie's crew lost an aileron in a thunderstorm on the fourth and last raid in the series. Currie was later to write a memorable book about his time at Wickenby, a book which was later translated into an equally successful TV documentary.

47. F/O Vallance and crew, 626 Squadron, Wickenby, 1945.

Twenty-five aircraft went to Peenemunde on August 17 and one, piloted by Sqdn Ldr Slade, the officer commanding A Flight, failed to return. Five more aircraft were lost before the end of the month. It was a grim time for the squadron. There was some respite in September when just four Lancasters were lost. One of them was flown by an Australian, Pilot Officer Hutchinson, who lost three engines after being attacked on his way back from a raid on Munich. His wireless operator managed to get a distress call off and later five of the crew, including the pilot, were picked up 60 miles off the Lincolnshire coast. Learning from this experience, the whole squadron was encouraged to practise dead-engine flying and dinghy drill and visits were arranged to the air sea rescue unit at Grimsby, Hutchinson's rescuers.

The first H2S-equipped aircraft arrived at Wickenby that month and an extensive training programme began on the new air-ground radar which was to begin a technology-led revolution in bombing.

Some crews appeared to be jinxed. Flt Lt Rowland was attacked by night-fighters in successive raids in October on Hanover. His rear gunner was killed in the first and three members of his crew injured in the second. Pilot Officer Hutchinson, the man rescued from the dinghy, brought a badly damaged Lancaster back from Frankfurt. In the same raid Pilot Officer Currie, who lost an aileron over Hamburg, had his aircraft hit by bombs from another Lancaster and had to crash land at West Malling. The following month Hutchinson, who by now had transferred to 626 Squadron, crashed at the same airfield after being shot up by a night-fighter over Berlin. He was later promoted to Flying Officer but failed to return on the 30th and last op of his tour over Schweinfurt in February 1944.

626 Squadron came into being on November 7, 1943 and was formed from C Flight of 12 Squadron with Wing Commander P. Haynes as its first CO.

Both squadrons had a bad night over Berlin on November 26. Three 12 Squadron aircraft were so badly damaged they were written off on their return to Wickenby. 626 lost one crew while a second overshot while trying a forced landing at Marham and four of the crew were killed. And a third was wrecked after a heavy landing at Wickenby.

Four aircraft were lost in a raid on Berlin on December 2, including a 626 flight commander, and two more crashed coming back from the same target two weeks later, one killing six and fatally injuring the seventh member of the crew when it came down at Hainton, near Market Rasen.

48. PH-U of 12 Squadron, early 1945.

49. ***above:*** *12 Squadron's King Kong and crew, late 1944.*
50. ***below:*** *S. Black and crew, 12 Squadron, Wickenby, late 1944.*

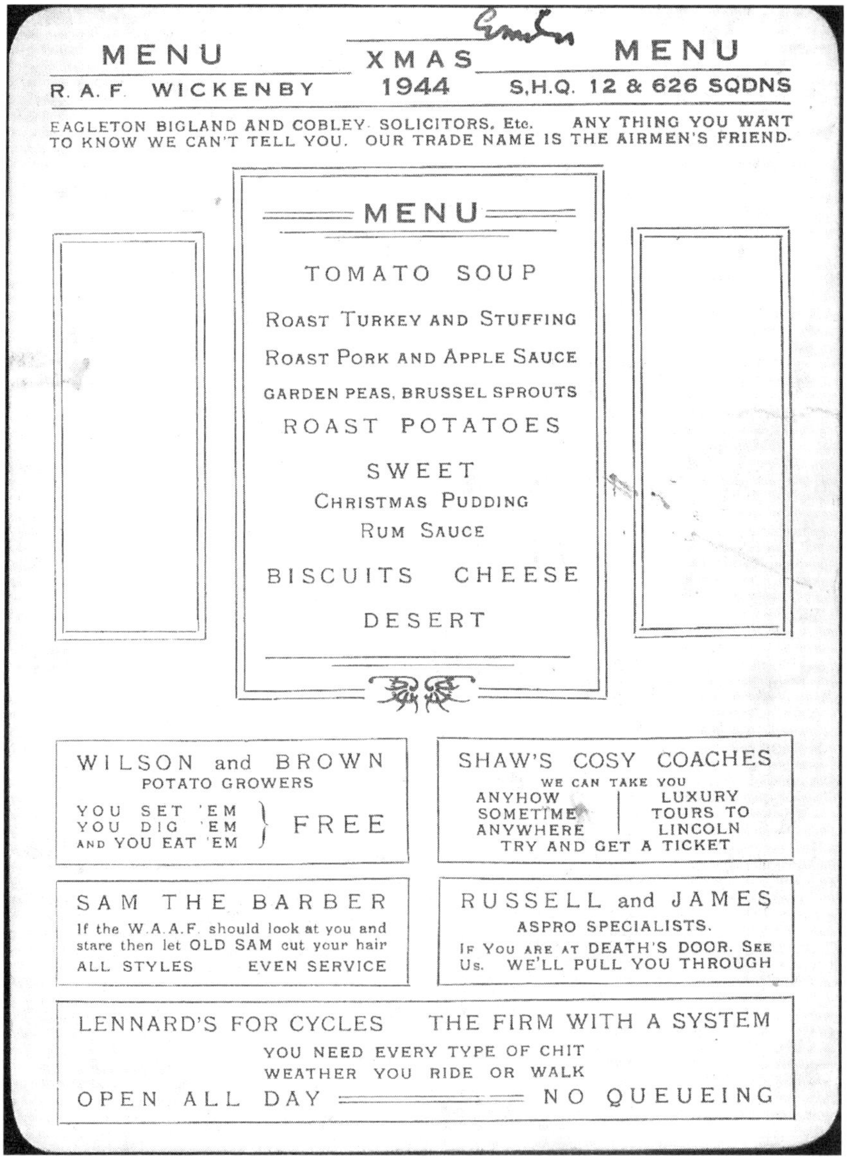

MENU XMAS MENU

R. A. F. WICKENBY 1944 S.H.Q. 12 & 626 SQDNS

EAGLETON BIGLAND AND COBLEY. SOLICITORS, Etc. ANY THING YOU WANT TO KNOW WE CAN'T TELL YOU. OUR TRADE NAME IS THE AIRMEN'S FRIEND.

MENU

TOMATO SOUP

ROAST TURKEY AND STUFFING

ROAST PORK AND APPLE SAUCE

GARDEN PEAS, BRUSSEL SPROUTS

ROAST POTATOES

SWEET

CHRISTMAS PUDDING

RUM SAUCE

BISCUITS CHEESE

DESERT

WILSON and BROWN
POTATO GROWERS
YOU SET 'EM
YOU DIG 'EM } FREE
AND YOU EAT 'EM

SHAW'S COSY COACHES
WE CAN TAKE YOU
ANYHOW | LUXURY
SOMETIME | TOURS TO
ANYWHERE | LINCOLN
TRY AND GET A TICKET

SAM THE BARBER
If the W.A.A.F. should look at you and stare then let OLD SAM cut your hair
ALL STYLES EVEN SERVICE

RUSSELL and JAMES
ASPRO SPECIALISTS.
IF YOU ARE AT DEATH'S DOOR. SEE US. WE'LL PULL YOU THROUGH

LENNARD'S FOR CYCLES THE FIRM WITH A SYSTEM
YOU NEED EVERY TYPE OF CHIT
WEATHER YOU RIDE OR WALK
OPEN ALL DAY NO QUEUEING

*51. **right:** Christmas Menu 1944 at RAF Wickenby.*

*52. **below:** This superb photograph of 12 Squadron crews and Lancasters was taken in January 1944 for the Illustrated magazine. A Press day had been held at Ludford but, because of the secrecy of its ABC-equipped Lancasters, the photographs of the aircraft were actually taken at Wickenby.*

Sgt Stavant and his crew had a baptism of fire when they flew their first op on December 29 when again Berlin was the target. They were attacked by a fighter but fought back and managed to escape. On their second trip three nights later, again to Berlin, they were attacked again and this time claimed to have destroyed the night-fighter.

One of the two aircraft lost by 12 Squadron on January 5 in a raid on Stettin was that of Flt Lt Bedford. His aircraft had been damaged over the target and ran out of fuel over the North Sea. The wireless operator managed to get off an accurate "fix" for the rescue services and Bedford managed to ditch. Coastal Command and air sea rescue launches were sent out immediately and later that morning a dinghy containing Bedford and his crew was spotted. The Coastal Command aircraft dropped a bigger dinghy for them and eventually they were picked up by a warship, HMS Midge. The crew were sent on leave when they returned to Wickenby. They were back in time to take part in a raid on Berlin on January 27 and were all lost when their aircraft was shot down.

Pilot Officer Currie's crew, whose aircraft had been hit by lightning and by falling bombs, was one of three 626 Squadron crews who beat the odds and completed their tour in yet another Berlin raid on January 29. Currie's rear gunner, Sgt Brettell, completed his second tour at the same time. There was quite a party at Wickenby that night.

Thirty aircraft were sent for the first time from Wickenby for the Schweinfurt raid in February, a month which was to cost the two squadrons nine aircraft. It didn't take a mathematical genius to work out what the odds against crews surviving were at this time.

March saw a record 36 Lancasters sent to a single target, Stuttgart. It was a record to be broken two raids later when 37 aircraft bombed Frankfurt. Two nights later six of the 29 Lancasters sent to Berlin were lost, one flown by 626's new CO, Wing Cmdr Quentin Ross, who had only taken over his new post three weeks earlier.

The Nuremburg raid at the end of the month cost 12 Squadron two Lancasters with three others damaged, while 626 was one of the few squadrons taking part in that disastrous raid to escape relatively unscathed, only one of the 16 aircraft it sent being damaged.

As the emphasis began to switch away from Germany to France in April, casualties at Wickenby dropped sharply. April saw only four aircraft lost though several others were badly damaged and brought back dead or injured crew members. 12 Squadron's X-Xray, for instance, was hit by flak over Friedrichshafen and came back to Wickenby with one engine virtually shot away, the throttle controls out of action and a rear turret badly damaged.

During that month the two Wickenby squadrons between them dropped over 1,200 tons of bombs, a figure which was to be exceeded month after month that summer as Bomber Command's might was thrown against the French railway system, the German army in Normandy and the rocket sites along the French coast.

It was a campaign which was to begin disastrously for both Wickenby squadrons. On the night of May 3 Bomber Command sent 346 Lancasters from 1 and 5 Groups to bomb a German military camp at Mailly-le-Camp, near Paris. Confusion over the target, faulty marking and interference of radio reception led to most of the aircraft being ordered to orbit for 15 minutes. This allowed time for the night-fighters to arrive and 42 Lancasters were shot down — seven of them from Wickenby. 12 Squadron lost four, 626 three. Seven other 12 Squadron aircraft returned damaged, two claiming to have shot down night-fighters.

June saw the Wickenby squadrons drop almost 2,300 tons of bombs in 18 raids, most supporting the Allied landings in Normandy. For one attack on the refineries at Gelsenkirchen, they dispatched 42 aircraft, a figure which was not to be surpassed during the war. The cost in June was nine Lancasters, one ditching and four being lost in one attack on railway yards near Orleans. In July three were lost in an attack on Courtrai and the same number in a raid on Karlsruhe while August saw five lost on operations and two other Lancasters crashing, killing 10 of the 14 men on board.

Only two aircraft were lost in September but the two massed raids on Duisburg on October 14 cost Wickenby six Lancasters, five shot down and another ditching in the sea near Grimsby.

In an attack on Stuttgart, 12 Squadron's A-Able was attacked by a fighter and dived out of control. The pilot, Flying Officer W.J. Buchan, ordered his crew to bail out but managed to regain control, not before two of his crew had taken to their parachutes.

On October 29 the Wickenby Lancasters were ordered to go in at 2,000ft in a raid on German forces on the island of Walcheren. When they returned several aircraft were found to have been damaged by bomb splinters.

The sheer scale of Bomber Command operations now had surpassed anything that had gone before. That October 626 Squadron dropped 1,225 tons of bombs, 12 Squadron 1,151. Wickenby now had an establishment of 1,754 men and women, and remember this was just one of 14 airfields

53. ***above:*** *Squadron Leader Villiers of 12 Squadron, March 1943.*
54. ***below:*** *Canadians at Wickenby. Sgt Hannah and F/Sgt McDevitt of 12 Squadron pictured at one of the accommodation sites, April 1944. Sgt Hannah was later wounded.*

55. **above:** *Wireless op at work in a 626 Lancaster, late 1944.*
56. **below:** *Flt Lt Joe Lancaster and namesake, 12 Squadron, Wickenby, early 1943.*

then forming part of 1 Group.

November proved to be a frustrating time for the aircrews at Wickenby. Time and time again they were briefed for raids, their aircraft bombed up only for the operation to be scrubbed, often by the time they had boarded their aircraft. It was much the same story in December as bad weather curtailed much operational flying.

On December 18, for instance, both squadrons were warned for an attack in support of ground troops in Holland. At 9.30am the following morning the crews were briefed. At 11.20 the raid was postponed until 15.00 only to be cancelled altogether 45 minutes later. Then at 16.30 17 aircraft were ordered to be ready as the op was back on again. At 7.30am the following morning, 17 crews were briefed but at 9.45am the op was scrubbed yet again. By 16.20 both squadrons had been warned of a new raid planned for the following day.

There was a near disaster for the whole station on December 22 when a 626 Lancaster developed an engine problem on take-off for a raid on Koblenz. With more Lancasters taking off the pilot was ordered to head for Leeming in North Yorkshire but his aircraft suddenly went out of control and crashed in the bomb dump bays. There was a huge explosion as the Lancaster with its full load went up. The station records speak of an "enormous" crater and the good fortune the whole camp had that the Lancaster did not hit the dump itself. No trace of any of the seven men on board was found.

Three armourers were killed in an accident in the bomb dump in January, a month most remember at Wickenby for the bitter cold. Everyone, and that included aircrew, was ordered out on snow clearing operations several times during the month as Bomber Command refused to let the appalling weather prevent operations taking place.

A 1 Group daylight raid on Neuss in late February was ordered with 12 Squadron to lead all 14 Base aircraft. This necessitated the fins and rudders of their Lancasters being painted white, the idea being that when they bombed, everyone else followed suit. Out over the North Sea, the raid was aborted, the aircraft ordered to jettison their 4,000lb bombs in the North Sea and return to base. Back at Wickenby ground crew was ordered to remove all the white paint immediately!

It was evident that the war was almost over but there were some cruel reminders for the Wickenby squadrons in March that, although Germany was in its death throes, it was still capable of fighting back. 12 Squadron lost eight aircraft in the month, six in one raid on Nuremburg

57. ***opposite page:*** *12 Squadron tanker and corporals, Wickenby, August 1944.*

58. ***above:*** *12 Squadron's Minnie the Moocher pictured over a V1 site, July/August 1944.*

59. ***left:*** *Johnny Oram at the controls of a 626 Squadron Lancaster, late 1944.*

60. ***above:*** *Wickenby's Maintenance Wing, winners of the 1 Group cup final, 1944-45.*
61. ***below:*** *A 626 Squadron crew pictured after completing their tour at Wickenby in 1945. They are (back row, from the left): S. Hall, A. Ward, J. McDonald, D. Wells; (front) D. Joss, F/O A. Wood and J. Wales.*

(although two were later found to have landed safely in France). 626 lost a Lancaster in the same raid.

The final losses for both squadrons came in a night attack on the refinery at Lutzkendorf on April 4, 12 Squadron losing one aircraft and 626 two. The raid itself was mounted by over 270 aircraft, mostly 1 Group Lancasters, at a cost of six aircraft, half of them from Wickenby.

There was a distinguished visitor at the end of the month when Lord Trenchard visited Wickenby and inspected the squadrons, 12 Squadron one of the oldest in the RAF and 1 Group's senior Squadron and 626, very much a representative of the wartime expansion of Bomber Command.

Wickenby didn't last long as a bomber airfield once the war was over. 12 Squadron moved to Binbrook in July and 626 was disbanded at Wickenby that October.

But much of the airfield remains. Binbrook apart (which was operational until 1988), it is perhaps the best preserved of the 1 Group airfields and is still used by light aircraft.

62. Air and ground crew of Colin Henry's Lancaster of 12 Squadron. This aircraft ditched in the North Sea on October 14, 1944 after an engine failure and the crew were picked up by the Grimsby ASR launch.

*63. **above:** Pictured with a veteran. Assorted aircrew with N-Nan, showing 106 operational symbols, Wickenby.*

*64. **below:** N.L. Howlett, with air and ground crew, 626 Squadron, late 1944.*

A Bad Winter

GEORGE WOODHEAD and his crew didn't have far to go when they finished their Heavy Conversion Unit course at Faldingworth in the early autumn of 1943 — they were posted just three miles to Wickenby where 626 Squadron was just forming.

They had had a pretty miserable time at Faldingworth. The HCU had moved in well before the airfield was finished and there was little but runways, flying control, a few scattered buildings and acres of mud.

"Wickenby wasn't a great deal better although our own billets were quite good," said Mr Woodhead. "626 had the wooden huts on the Fulnetby-Rand road while 12 Squadron were towards Holton Beckering."

He was a mid-upper gunner and his was one of the founder crews of 626. They flew operationally for the first time on the Modane raid on November 11/12 and went on to complete 16 trips with 626 before joining a Pathfinder squadron at Warboys.

"It was a very bad winter for Bomber Command," recalled Mr Woodhead. "There were some very tough raids that winter. We did nine on Berlin alone. One of the worst was the night we were hit by bad winds and were blown right over the Ruhr defences. And on another our aircraft, V-Victor, wouldn't climb above 17,000 feet and we arrived half an hour after everyone else and came back across Denmark in daylight, but we got away with it. That aircraft had done 80 raids when we got it but I believe it later went to a training unit and survived the war."

It was not long after they left 626 that they were shot down, their Lancaster being hit by flak over Dusseldorf. The rear gunner was killed instantly but the other six all escaped by parachute. George Woodhead believes three of them, the bomb-aimer, navigator and flight engineer, were lynched by enraged German civilians soon after they landed.

"I was the last out of the plane," he said. "I landed 10 miles from the target, the wireless operator and skipper six miles and eight miles away. I believe the first three landed in or near Dusseldorf and were lynched. I know I nearly was myself.

"After I was captured I was taken into Dusseldorf and we stopped at a cross-roads and they were bringing dead and injured out of a building. When we reached a police control centre one of the wardens saw me and went berserk. He grabbed me by the throat and tried to throttle me but was dragged away by the chief warden."

He spent four days at a nearby airfield and then he and five other downed RAF men were taken to a PoW centre. They needed a dozen guards to ensure their safe passage, yet there were still some ugly moments for them.

"With hindsight, it is easy to see why this sort of thing happened," said Mr Woodhead, who still lives in his home town of Gainsborough.

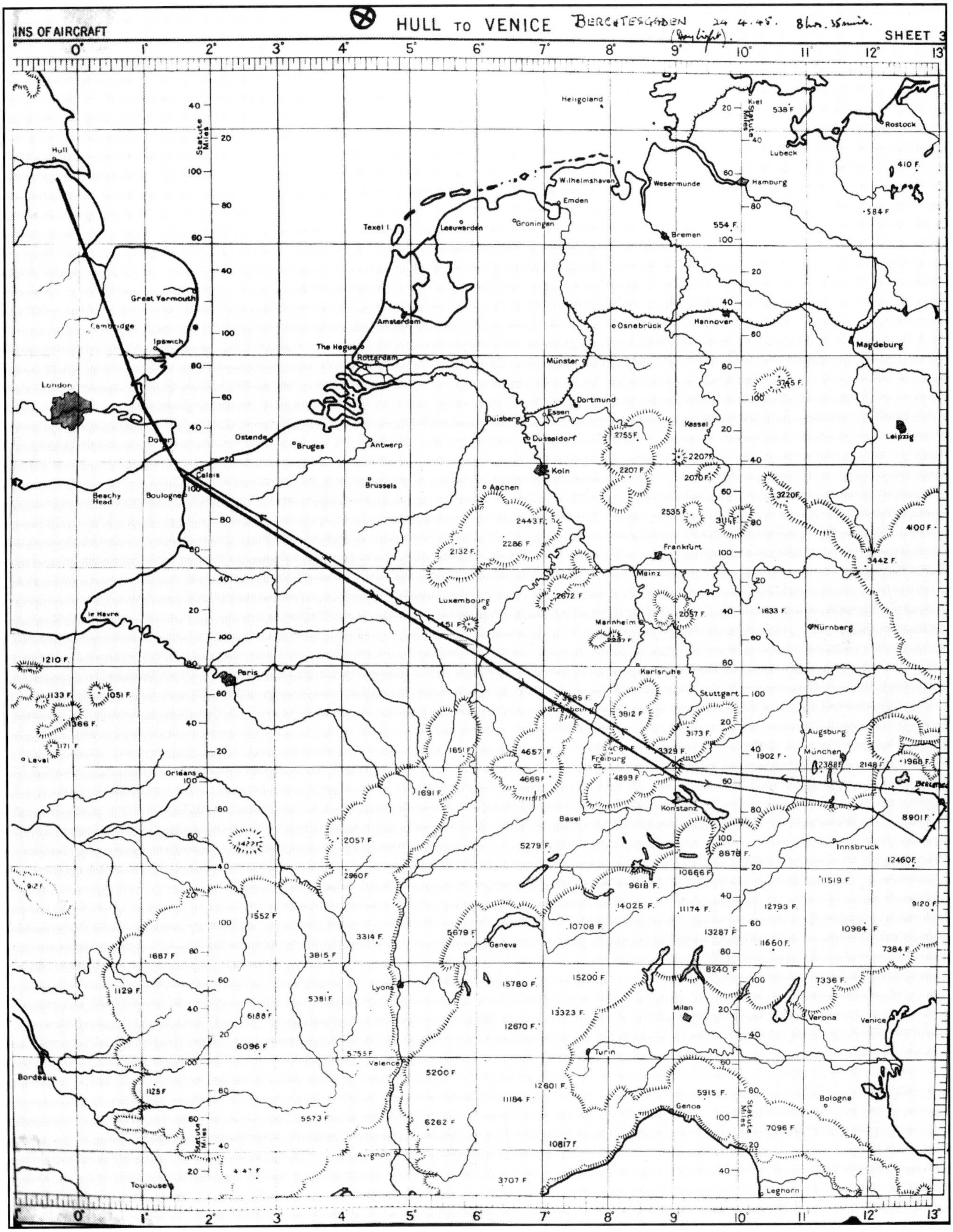

65. **opposite page, above:** *The last raid. 1 and 5 Group Lancasters pictured over the Bavarian Alps on the last raid on Germany on April 25, 1945.*

66. **opposite page, below:** *An unidentified but well-used Lancaster pictured over Berchtesgarten on April 25, 1945, the last raid of the war on a German target. It was almost exclusively a Lincolnshire affair with 359 Lancasters, mainly from 1 and 5 Groups, bombing the SS barracks.*

67. **above:** *This was the route map for that last raid issued to crews of 166 Squadron at Kirmington.*

Brothers

We shared a common bond throughout those
Wartime years, for we were young and together,
Shared the doubts and fears of war.
How well we came to know that world within
A world wherein we lived; from day to day, and
Far apart from other fighting men; who fought
As we did, a common foe.
Vast was our arena: The darkening light at
Dusk, the snarling roar of laden Lancs; the lethal
Night time skies; the onrushing hours that claimed
Our Youth; and we were so aware that we might die
Before sweet dawn.
And so we knew death and lived o'er long with fear.
Although there were those amongst us who did not
Care. But often, they who laugh the loudest fear
The most.
***So** night after searing night we flew into hell as*
Brothers; to find that the Reaper was our grinning Host.

John Walsh, November, 1988

Kirmington's Proud Record

HUMBERSIDE AIRPORT is one of the fastest growing regional airports in the United Kingdom, but it owes its very existence to the rapid expansion of 1 Group of Bomber Command in the early war years.

The airport at Kirmington was the Phoenix which rose from the ashes of a wartime bomber station, almost exclusively the home of 166 Squadron of 1 Group. It was one of the first wave of new airfields, opened to permitted limited flying in January 1942, although it was to wait for a year before becoming an operational bomber station.

It was the ideal site for a bomber airfield when the Air Ministry surveyors were looking around in 1940 and proved to be the ideal site when the old Lindsey County Council looked for somewhere to develop a North Lincolnshire airport 30 years later.

The village of Kirmington stands on a small flat plain just to the east of where the Lincolnshire Wolds peter out on their northward march to the Humber. Along with its topographical benefits went its proximity to Barnetby railway station and the A18 trunk road, which actually cut through the northern end of the main runway. Traffic on the Grimsby to Scunthorpe road was re-routed through Croxton but the old A18 was still used by local traffic. At the point where it intersected the runway an armed guard was mounted and his job when flying was taking place (as it seemed to be most of the time from the summer of 1943 onwards) was to drag barbed wire barriers across the road and make sure no one crossed.

Kirmington's 150ft wide paved runways were amongst the first to be laid in 1 Group and their familiar A-pattern was supplemented by dispersals for 37 aircraft. The runways were laid during the latter part of 1941, the first area of the airfield to be completed. While the work was still going on the main runway was being used by Oxfords and Ansons from 21 Group Flying Training Command. The contractors in the meantime were busy working on the first accommodation areas, the technical sites and erecting the first of the three T2 hangars.

The initial accommodation sites were close to the airfield but the occasional sortie by German intruder aircraft brought about a rethink at Bawtry Hall and it was decided to move the living accommodation to dispersed sites on the edge of Brocklesby Park some distance from the airfield. Bicycles became obligatory at RAF Kirmington.

It was finally handed over to Bomber Command as a satellite of Elsham Wolds in October 1942 and its first occupants were to be 150 Squadron, one of the original 1 Group units, which moved in from Snaith at the end of the month. 150 was to remain at Kirmington for less than two months and on December 12 sent 12 of its Wellingtons to Blida in North Africa. At the same time 142

68. A crew which served with both 103 and 166 Squadrons, pictured probably at Elsham. They are (back row): C. Jackson, rear gunner, K. Cave, bomb-aimer, P. Chesterton, pilot, A. Robson, mid-upper gunner; (front) H. Ackroyd, flight engineer, Jack Bullock, wireless operator, and Ted Milling, navigator.

Squadron, which was based at Waltham, sent a similar number of its aircraft to North Africa and the remainder of the squadron moved to Kirmington where, in January 1943, it merged with the home echelon of 150 to reform 166 Squadron.

166 had first seen action in 1918 as one of the then-new RAF bomber squadrons. It was disbanded the following year but reformed in 1936 only to disappear again in 1940 as part of a merger leading to the formation of No 10 Operational Training Unit. Now 166 was back again, this time as a front-line bomber squadron which, over the next two years and four months, was to drop 27,000 tons of bombs and 300 mines. Its members were to win two DSOs, two CGMs, 117 DFCs and 108 DFMs.

The newest squadron in Bomber Command lost no time in going into action. The very night it was formed mines were laid off the German coast and two nights later 12 Wellingtons took part in a largely inconclusive raid on Lorient.

That spring and summer 166 was to send its Wellingtons out on 43 bombing raids and 33 mining operations, an indication of how much emphasis was being put on anti-shipping operations in those early days. Those raids were to cost the squadron 39 aircraft, a loss rate of five per cent. This meant the average crew could expect to last for 19 or 20 operations. There is little wonder that few of those original 166 airmen survived the war. The Grim Reaper certainly did his work amongst the young men from Kirmington that summer.

The raids on Hamburg in July cost 166 five Wellingtons, four shot down and one crashing on take-off. Twenty airmen died.

In September the squadron converted to Lancasters, taking over aircraft which had previously been used by 103 Squadron at Elsham. Their first raid in their new aircraft was to Hanover on September 22 when five American B-17s from the 8th Air Force went along to sample night operations. They chose to stick to day-time flying.

166 was to bear its share of the heavy losses suffered by Bomber Command that autumn. Berlin was the major target as winter approached and there was a particularly tragic end to a raid on December 16 when the squadron lost two Lancasters and 14 men when the returning bombers found North Lincolnshire shrouded in low cloud and fog.

At a minute to midnight Lancaster LM395, which had taken off from Kirmington eight hours

69. ***opposite page:*** *A Wellington III pictured with the A Flight ground staff at Kirmington in 1943.*
70. ***above:*** *Kirmington soon after the war had finished. Note the dark, oil-stained dispersals.*

earlier, emerged from low cloud and struck high ground at Caistor. There were no survivors. The pilot was Sgt Stan Miller from Scarborough. He had been married barely four months and was later to be buried in his home town. His crew, Sgts T. Rudden, H. Hine, H. Miles, B. Haney, J. Murphy and W. Allen, all died with him.

At around the same time, a second Kirmington Lancaster, S-Sugar, piloted by Sgt A. Brown, crashed in open land between Elsham and Goxhill. Again, there were no survivors from the seven-man crew.

Harsh weather curtailed flying in the first month of 1944 and into February. The station records note that on February 10, when there was no flying, a parade was held in blizzard conditions. "It is noteworthy," said the records, "that the flight commanders had no idea how to look after their men."

That same record clerk noted that on February 15 166 lost two aircraft and their crews over Berlin, followed by three more four nights later on a Leipzig raid.

By now work had been completed on the sodium lighting ring around Kirmington and, on a good night, homecoming crews were said to be able to see the airfield from 50 miles away. It was also decided to use red lights to illuminate Pelham's Pillar, the monument standing on top of the Wolds a few miles south of Kirmington, as an additional beacon.

A measure of the determination of 1 Group at this time to make sure every possible bomber could fly was demonstrated at Kirmington early on the morning of February 27. Heavy snow was falling and with ops likely that night the whole of the station staff, including the aircrew, was turned out at 4.30am to begin snow clearing operations. By mid-day the runways had been cleared, but then a planned raid on Munich was scrubbed. The station records commented: "With adequate equipment and manpower it is possible to keep a bomber station open in these conditions." But it was stressed that those involved in the operation should be fortified with a hot drink every hour.

The Battle of Berlin was costing 166 Squadron dearly. The final raid of the 16 in which the squadron participated took place on March 24. Four aircraft were lost that night, bringing the squadron's losses for the raids to 17 of the 270 dispatched, a loss rate in excess of six per cent. It was the highest missing rate in 1 Group and cost the lives of 109 men while another 24 became prisoners.

It could have been even worse. On the afternoon of that final raid one aircraft, ND625, was

71. B Flight groundstaff, 166 Squadron.

being bombed up at Kirmington when the full bomb load was jettisoned on the ground while checks were being carried out. The duty rigger, L/AC Bishop, moved quickly to kick away a number of incendiaries which had ignited. His actions certainly saved the Lancaster and probably the four others on nearby dispersals.

The Nuremburg raid at the end of March was another disaster for 166 with four of the 20 Lancasters sent failing to return. Those lost all fell victim to night-fighters.

To make matters worse, three of the aircraft were carrying an eighth crew member, possibly newcomers to the squadron flying on ops to gain experience. It was quite usual in some squadrons for new pilots to go as "second dickey" before they took their own crew.

The first of the 166 Lancasters to go down that night was flown by Pilot Officer W. Burnett. He died but three of his crew escaped as the Lancaster crashed near Bonn. The only one of the four pilots to survive was Flt Lt Taylor, whose aircraft was brought down near Weidenhahn, two crew members being killed. The third to crash was the Lancaster flown by Sgt R. Fennell. It came down on the airfield at Giessen and only one of the crew escaped. The fourth 166 Lancaster to be lost was piloted by Flt Lt Proctor and was brought down near Fulda; all eight men on board died. All four aircraft are likely to have been shot down by night-fighters using upward-firing cannon, a weapon which was to claim so many RAF bombers during 1944.

It wasn't just enemy action which killed the young men (and one or two young women) at Kirmington. There were a number of fatal road accidents around the airfield that spring including one in which an ATS officer died at Habrough. Because the accommodation sites were so dispersed and so many relied on bicycles, the chances of accidents rose steeply on dark nights with vehicles unable to use all but the dimmest lights.

There was a remarkable incident at Kirmington on April 10 as Lancasters were taking off for an attack on the railway yards at Aulnoye. Four aircraft were already airborne when F-Fox came to grief. It seems a tyre may have burst for the bomber, carrying 14 1,000lb bombs, swerved off the runway and within a minute or so caught fire. The crew scrambled clear before at least nine of the bombs on board exploded, completely destroying F-Fox, damaging four aircraft nearby and leaving a crater 50ft wide and 15ft deep which later needed 500 tons of rubble and soil to repair. Seventeen aircraft were unable to take off and those that did had to land away after the raid as Kirmington was officially out of action.

By six o'clock the next morning 100 men were at work and within four and a half hours the runway was reported to be usable and the station was fully open again by 8pm that evening.

The blast from the bombs had also blown in the doors of the nearest hangar and it was later found that 500 panes of glass had been broken in Kirmington village.

Seventeen aircraft were able to operate the following night for an attack on Aachen, but there was to be a sequel for in mid-May it was found there was major subsidence at the point on the runway where the explosion had occurred and Kirmington was closed for flying until more substantial repairs could be carried out.

The disaster at Mailly-le-Camp, when 1 Group aircraft got a terrible mauling from the night-fighters, cost 166 three Lancasters with three more being lost in raids on Orleans and Aachen.

On May 22 a Lancaster returning from a raid on Dortmund came in with two dead engines, overshot and crashed in flames at the side of the airfield. The crash team was led by the station commander, Group Captain H.R. Graham, and arrived to find all the crew had escaped. Two days later the group captain handed over control at Kirmington to his successor, Group Captain G. Carter.

Raids on the railway yards at Aachen and the Nordstern oil plant at Gelsenkirchen either side of the D-Day landings cost 166 five Lancasters and heralded the start of a busy and punishing summer for the Kirmington squadron.

Their first daylight raid came along with most of 1 Group on Le Havre on June 14, and at the end of the month 166 put up a record 29 Lancasters for an attack on V1 sites in Northern France. One was lost. Another was shot down in the mass raid on Caen early in June and one of 166's worst nights of the war was to come five nights later. 1 Group was sent to the railway yards at Revigny but when they arrived they found the target obscured by cloud and well defended. Only half the aircraft bombed and 166 lost four out of the 10 Lancasters shot down.

Two nights later 1 Group was sent back to Revigny to finish the job. Kirmington's J-Jig burst a tyre and crashed on take-off, the crew escaping before it caught fire. This time the bomb load did not go up. There was a further mishap after a Stuttgart raid later in the month when A-Able pancaked on the runway and the two aircraft left to land had to be diverted to one of the neighbouring 1 Group airfields.

72. AS-F with air and ground crew at Kirmington in 1945. This was another aircraft with a forward-mounted dorsal turret.

73. **above:** *Note the rather unusual cart just in front of the H2S dome on this Mk III Lancaster at Kirmington in 1944.*
74. **below:** *All aboard a Wellington. 166 personnel at Kirmington during the summer of 1943.*

There was quite a party at the end of June to mark the completion of the tour of Flying Officer Hutchinson and his crew. The station commander had gone along with them on their 30th trip, a daylight raid on Le Havre. No doubt some of the celebrations spilled over into the Kirmington squadron's local, the Marrowbone and Cleaver, known to all as the Chopper, which is still the scene of the squadron's reunions.

August was a bad month for 166 with eight aircraft lost, three against V1 sites, two in a raid on Kiel, one over Bordeaux and one on a mining sortie into the Baltic. The eighth aircraft, the successor to J-Jig, which had crashed and burnt out in June, came down in the sea after a mid-air collision with another aircraft from the squadron.

A raid on Neuss claimed the only two aircraft 166 lost in September but five were lost the

75. Sgt Stanley Miller of Scarborough who was killed when his 166 Squadron aircraft crashed in fog at Caistor returning to Kirmington on the night of December 16, 1943.

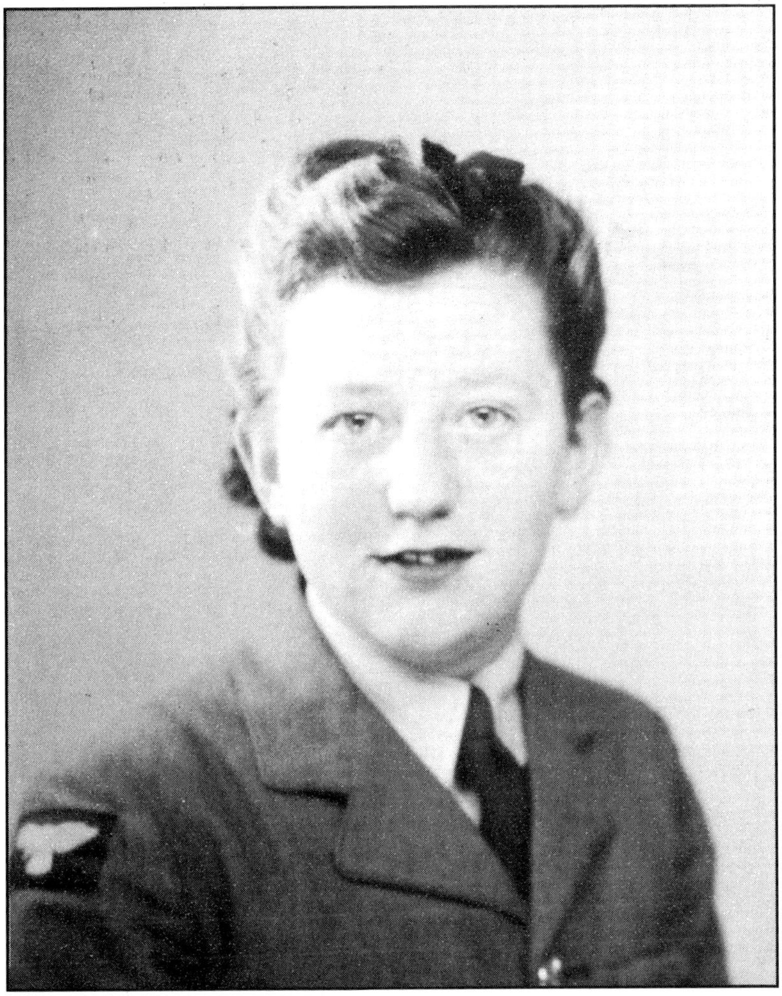

76. ***left:*** *LACW Pearl Cooper-Rawlings, who was a telephonist with 166 Squadron from December 1943 until the squadron's disbandment.*

77. ***below:*** *The crew of AS-C at Kirmington. They are (from the left): Bill Short, bomb-aimer, Jim Wright, wireless operator, Gordon Bannatine RNZAF, navigator, Chas Martin RNZAF, pilot, Jake Bracey, rear gunner, Harry Kelly, mid-upper gunner and David Eaves, flight engineer.*

78. ***right:*** *LACW Louise Styles, 166 Squadron.*

79. ***below:*** *The news of the D-Day landings is broken to 166 aircrew by Flt Lt Frank Tighe, the station adjutant. On the left is the squadron CO, Wing Commander Don Garner DSO. Among the group is F/O Donald Pleasance, later to become one of the country's best-known actors. He was the wireless operator to F/O Tutty when they were shot down over Agenville on August 31 and spent the rest of the war as a PoW.*

80. ***above:*** *The Station Band at Kirmington.*

81. ***left:*** *LACW Kathlyn Andrews, who worked in the Sergeants' Mess at RAF Kirmington from July 1944 to May 1946.*

82. ***above:*** *Jacko Jackson and his crew, 166 Squadron. The others are rear gunner Ted Hopkins, W. Mault, the mid-upper, R. Fox, navigator, A. Gordon, engineer, Jock Gillies, wireless operator, and John Russell, bomb-aimer.*
83. ***below:*** *The final parade at Kirmington on the disbandment of 166 Squadron, November 1945. Taking the salute is Wing Commander T.W. Hodgson.*
84. ***opposite page, right:*** *166 Squadron, September 1943.*

following month, including one which crashed at Hemswell while on a fighter affiliation exercise. There were 10 men on board, the normal crew plus three "spare" gunners. There were no survivors.

There was a new squadron at Kirmington that month when 166's C Flight was detached to reform 153 Squadron, which had flown Defiants and Beaufighters earlier in the war. It operated from Kirmington for a few days, providing 11 of the 31 aircraft sent to Emmerich on October 7, before leaving for Scampton. It was replaced by a new 166 C Flight which had formed at Faldingworth.

The rear gunner of F-Freddie was killed in a battle with a night-fighter over Dusseldorf and two nights later a raid on Bochum cost the squadron yet another Lancaster and its seven-man crew. The same raid also saw P-Peter crash short of the airfield at Croxton, the rear gunner being taken to hospital in Grimsby where he died later. Raids on Duren and Freiburg each cost the squadron a Lancaster, the latter being the only 1 Group aircraft lost on this raid.

Freiburg was a small town which had previously been untouched in the bombing war. 1 Group crews were told that night it was an important railway centre and contained many German troops massing to repel the advances of the nearby American and French forces.

1 Group's AOC, Air Vice Marshal Sir Edward Rice, later sent a congratulatory message to his squadrons on their efforts in dispatching 312 aircraft against this target, the most ever sent in one raid by any of Bomber Command's eight Groups. It was, he said, a splendid achievement, the aircraft dropping 1,900 tons of bombs on the town. Freiburg, in the meantime, had been absolutely devastated, although the railway was not hit. Of the 3,000 who died that night, it is believed only 75 were German troops.

Four aircraft were lost in December, one over Karlsruhe and two over Cologne on Christmas Eve. The fourth was X-Xray flown by Flying Officer Hanna. Coming back from the Karlsruhe raid, it hit trees in Brocklesby Park and burnt out. There were no survivors.

In another incident, a Lancaster was damaged in an attack on the Leuna refinery, near Leipzig, and five of the crew baled out over France. The pilot, Flying Officer Lee, and his navigator remained with the aircraft and brought it back to Manston in Kent. Both were later decorated and all seven of the crew were reunited within a short period at Kirmington.

The first raid of 1945, on January 2 on Nuremburg, cost the squadron two Lancasters while the rear gunner of a third baled out. It was the beginning of a tough final four months of the war for 166 with 14 more Lancasters being lost up to April 4 when organised resistance began to crumble.

It was to provide a savage finale for 166 Squadron and for Kirmington as a military base, with 166 sometimes sending as many as 33 Lancasters on raids deep into Germany. The squadron remained at Kirmington until the early autumn when it was disbanded at Elsham Wolds, and the airfield itself was later used for several of the huge War Ministry disposal sales before the land between the runways was returned to agriculture.

Some 20 years later aircraft started using Kirmington again regularly and in the early 1970s Lindsey County Council, with some help from British Steel, redeveloped the airfield and opened it as North Lincolnshire Airport. A few days later it passed to the new Humberside authority and is now very successful, with a major runway extension planned.

Johnny Boy

Warm gold this day, so blue the sky;
and proud the blue you wore;
A pilot's brevet on your breast
through hostile days of war.
May the times we had be ever bright,
your language quelled my tears;
Now here you stand at Runnymede,
my vigil through the years.

Your name among the thousands
etched clear into the stone;
'Twixt other names and many lives
though I know but yours alone.
Your memorial stands in tribute,
and I lament with saddened heart;
Do echo grief of other souls, who
were, like us, to part.

John Walsh, 1986

Defying all the Odds

CECIL BRYANT'S first tour of operations spanned almost two years, four squadrons and seemingly half the airfields in Lincolnshire.

It was a tour that defied all the odds. Statistically, a crew's most dangerous period was in their first five trips: Cec went through that stage several times with different crews. The average survival period was 14 trips, probably less in the Wellingtons in which he did part of that tour.

But he survived to complete 33 operational trips with 1 Group and went on to do another 18 in the later stages of the war with 100 Group.

His tour started long before he had got to a squadron. He was at 27 OTU at Finningley learning to operate a Wellington in battle conditions when Bomber Command ordered that every available aircraft should take part in a 1,000 bomber raid on Dusseldorf. And the OTU aircraft were needed to make up the numbers.

After completing that course he and his crew were posted to Swinderby where they found 50 Squadron in 5 Group just about to convert from their disliked Manchesters to the aircraft's new big brother, the Lancaster. The shortage of aircraft meant a switch to 1 Group and a posting to 142 Squadron at Grimsby, an airfield which was now universally known to aircrew (and to the local population) as Waltham.

The squadron was under notice to move from Binbrook to Blida in Tunisia but Cec was withdrawn from the posting when it was discovered he had a perforated ear drum. It was believed it had been caused by altitude changes while flying and he was immediately grounded for six months. He was made acting station warrant officer at Waltham, pending the reforming on December 15, 1942 of 100 Squadron.

He was with his new squadron for precisely 16 days before being posted again to 166 Squadron at Kirmington. When he arrived there he was told his ear problems required hospitalisation and he was sent to the RAF hospital at Rauceby, near Sleaford, for three months. Back at Kirmington in late March, he found he had been "loaned" to 199 Squadron, then flying Wellington IIIs from Ingham, a satellite of Hemswell.

After three operations from Ingham the crew found themselves pilotless. The pilot's wife had just had a baby and he had applied for compassionate leave. This was turned down but he went anyway and later refused to fly again. This resulted in him being declared LMF — lacking moral fibre — stripped of his rank and sent to the disciplinary centre at Sheffield.

"We were all sent back to the OTU at Hixon to find another pilot," he said. "He turned out to be another one who had been through the centre at Sheffield, but for different reasons."

85. A Spitfire VB pictured at Kelstern. It had been taking part in fighter affiliation exercises with 625 Squadron Lancasters and dropped in for a social call. The Spitfire probably came from one of the Lincolnshire fighter airfields, Digby and Kirton Lindsey.

Sgt Russell Marks was an Australian who seemed determined to live up to the "wild colonial boy" image which some of his countrymen brought with them on the boat from Sydney. His antics finally came to an end when he flew his Wellington at rooftop height the length of the high street at Mablethorpe.

After a spell at Sheffield, he was posted to Waltham where he was put in charge of the runway lighting, not the kind of action he had hoped to see when volunteering for the Royal Air Force. So he decided to do something about it. He simply rang the Air Ministry in London, asked to be put through to "the bloke in charge" and demanded to know if he thought it proper that a trained bomber pilot should be switching the runway lights on and off at Waltham. It worked and within a few weeks he was back in the driver's seat of a Wellington.

Cec Bryant crewed up with him when Marks was half way through his tour. He was a natural pilot and was awarded a DFM for his actions during one raid on Hamburg (the story of which is told in part one of Maximum Effort).

Later, when he had completed his tour, Marks turned down the opportunity of a return to Australia, transferred to the Royal Australian Air Force and did another tour on Lancasters with 460 Squadron at Binbrook. He finally completed the war as Flt Lt Marks with a DFC to go with his DFM.

By now 166 was converting to Lancasters and Cec Bryant found himself at Blyton to pick up a new crew. This time he was posted to 103 Squadron at Elsham Wolds. When they arrived they found the station in the grip of a dysentery outbreak.

"The CO at Elsham was keen on maximum effort so all the fit men were crewed up willy-nilly. Elsham lost three aircraft that night and between them they carried five of my new crew," he said. It was only after the war that Cec found that one of the crew he had known so briefly did survive as a PoW.

So it was back to Blyton again for yet another crew, all of whom had spent some time in hospital during 1943. The other thing they had in common was that they were all survivors and by April 1944 they had gone through Bomber Command's most savage period and emerged with a complete tour to their credit (Cec Bryant had, in fact, completed 33; after his 30th his pilot, Flt Lt Stan Arnfield, a former Battle of Britain fighter ace, asked the squadron CO if he could keep Sgt Bryant on until he completed his own tour. The request was granted. Arnfield was awarded the DFC on the completion of his tour. Five of his crew, including Sgt Bryant, received DFMs).

After a spell instructing, he volunteered for operations again and found himself posted to yet another of his old squadrons, 199, which was now with 100 Group, flying electronic counter measures Halifaxes. By now the war had changed dramatically.

"When I first started you started fighting when you got half way across the Wash and finished

No. 166 SQUADRON, R.A.
Ma

as you came in to land," said Mr Bryant, who settled in Cleethorpes after the war. "By now the front line started the other side of Holland, there was little flak and only a few fighters."

He finished the war with 199 but still looks upon himself as a 166 Squadron man.

"It was the best one of the lot I was with. I did most of my first tour with them and, while we had some rough times, it was a good squadron with a good spirit."

Kirmington, too, is still the wartime airfield he remembers with the greatest affection. Its accommodation was rudimentary (he was there during the early days and the latter period when the accommodation was moved to dispersed sites in what was known as Habrough Wood) but whenever he drives past it still stirs memories of comradeships, shared experiences and the moments of exhilaration all Bomber Command crews enjoyed when they landed back after a trip. Those and the hedge at the Caistor end of the main runway which he remembers their Wellington puncturing after one hairy landing!

86. **left:** *This was the armament section of 625 Squadron at Kelstern in July 1944.*

87. **below:** *166 Squadron, May 1945.*

88. ***left:*** *460 Squadron armourers pictured at Breighton in East Yorkshire in the late spring of 1943 before they moved to Binbrook.*

89. ***below:*** *End of their tour. Red Martin's crew pictured at Kirmington after completing their 30th operational sortie. They are (from the left, back row): Orlando De Freitas, bomb-aimer, George Hodgson, engineer, Bob Ansell, rear gunner, Tom Williams, wireless operator, Ron Martin, pilot, Mat Hudson, mid-upper gunner, and Jack Dunlop, navigator.*

90. ***left:*** *Electricians at Ludford, 1943/44.*

91. ***above:*** *Flt Lt J.H. Clark and crew of 460 Squadron at Binbrook. Third from the left is Bob Dunstan, a rear gunner who had lost a leg in North Africa earlier in the war and had volunteered to fly as a gunner.*

92. ***left:*** *R. Yuel's crew, 626 Squadron, Wickenby, March 1945.*

93 & 94. ***above left and right:*** *Two familiar faces from Kirmington. LACW Norah Pink, a radio operator from September 1943 to January 1946, and Cpl Thompson, known to everyone as Scottie, who worked in the Officer's Mess.*

95. ***left:*** *Party time at Binbrook. Smiling faces at an undated 460 Squadron dance.*

96. ***left:*** *Sqdn Ldr Mackie and crew, Kirmington.*

97. ***below:*** *Wickenby flying control, 1944.*

98. ***left:*** *The band gets in the mood at a 460 Squadron dance at Binbrook.*

99. ***above:*** *F/Sgt Jack Goulevitch sports a top hat on this delightful picture taken in front of his crew's 460 Squadron Lancaster. In civvy street he was an undertaker.*

100. ***right:*** *Flying Officer Hal Ollis of Vancouver and his 625 Squadron crew pictured at Scampton.*

101. ***above:*** *The dove of peace? Perhaps. This is one of a series of superb photographs taken at Binbrook in 1944 for the folks back in Australia. 460 Squadron was the first and premier Australian squadron in Bomber Command and was to drop the most bombs and suffer the highest losses of any squadron.*

102. ***left:*** *A rare colour picture of a 1 Group crew about to leave for a raid on Essen. It was taken at Binbrook on Sunday March 11, 1945 and shows the crew of O-Oboe pictured with their ground crew minutes before take-off.*

103. ***above:*** *Flt Lt Clem Koder pictured in the snow at Kelstern as he watched G-George being bombed up.*
104. ***below:*** *Have guns, ready to travel. Two un-named 625 Squadron members with the Brownings stripped from the rear turret of an A Flight Lancaster.*

A Pilot's Story

CLEM KODER was a Lancaster pilot who completed 36 operations with 1 Group between September 1944 and March 1944.

It was a tour of operations which earned Clem a DFC and which was completed in spite of the fact that his height (he was just over 5ft 4ins tall) meant he had been classified as unsuitable for heavy aircraft.

But he was something of a rarity. He was already a very experienced pilot when he went to his Operational Training Unit at Finningley, just outside Doncaster. He had spent the previous two years as a pilot with an Observers' Advanced Flying Unit in Cumberland, flying mainly Ansons and the occasional Defiant and Lysander.

It was a period which had provided him with a great deal of night and instrument flying, exactly what a good bomber pilot needed. He had gone through part of his OTU "headless", that is without a crew. He was intended for a Mosquito squadron and he would pick up his navigator later. But then he was called in by his CO and told there was a crew from 100 Squadron whose pilot had lost his nerve after three trips. They were looking for an experienced pilot to take them on. Clem agreed and, after a spell at Sandtoft, he was posted along with his new crew to 625 Squadron at Kelstern.

It was to be the start of a long association between Clem and one of Bomber Command's fledgling squadrons, an association which is as strong today as it was 45 years ago.

This is how Clem Koder remembers his time with 625 at Kelstern: "Duties with Flying Training Command, although a most necessary function, called for no relaxation but lacked the excitement and great spirit that one found on an operation squadron.

"Always when asked: 'Were you frightened on operations?' I would answer: 'No, I do not think so. I was more frightened that I would not keep up the high standard set by the squadron personnel.' This also applied to the ground crews whose servicing was of the highest quality at all times of the day and night regardless of the weather conditions. It was the magnificent spirit of all that helped me and I shall always feel proud to be one of those who operated in Bomber Command.

"I found it a great thrill to taxi out in my Lancaster, G-George, with others around the perimeter track to the runway and to be signalled onto the runway to prepare for take-off. Then we would be lined up, looking straight down the runway, brakes on with increasing revs, the whole aircraft shuddering, yearning to be released, and then, at the moment of take-off, away we went, backs pressed hard against our seats, a quick glance to port to give a wave to the Station Commander and others giving us an encouraging send-off.

"Very often take-off would be at dusk and the usual practice would be to circle base gradually to about 5,000 feet and as one did so 460 Squadron RAAF at Binbrook, some four miles to the west, could be seen similarly circling base and climbing. To the northwest 100 Squadron at Waltham, just south of Grimsby, could also be seen, and so too 101 Squadron could be seen at Ludford Magna, a few miles south of us, and beyond them was 170 Squadron at Dunholme Lodge.

"At 5,000 feet, the aircraft, still climbing, headed west of south for Reading, and in the fading light the concentration of Lancasters would be seen forming a long stream and picking up other squadrons from bases in South Lincolnshire and Huntingdonshire. At Reading there was still sufficient light to pick out many aircraft in the bomber stream as it turned to port in a south easterly direction to Beachy Head. By the time the Channel coast was reached the light had gone and so also had the comforting sight of all those other Lancasters.

"As the English coastline receded and the blackness of the water below took over, one felt somewhat isolated in spite of the confidence I had in my navigator, Hal Zlotnik, a Canadian from Vancouver, and the confidence in the navigators of the other aircraft I knew were nearby. Strangely enough, some of those navigators had been pupils of mine only months earlier at the Observers' AFU.

"After some 20 minutes, the blackness below would be broken by the pale line formed by a sandy beach or a chalk white cliff on the French coast, some 17,000 or 18,000 feet below. Still feeling out on one's own, a check with Hal seemed necessary. As usual he gave me the assurance I was looking for — we were on track.

"Time went on and through the darkness no friendly aircraft appeared to be keeping us company. At about 20 minute intervals I called up Hal for the usual check and while I received the comforting response, he knew my reason for doing so.

"After three or perhaps four hours, there was suddenly 30 seconds to H-Hour and the first illuminators could be seen falling over the target area to be followed by the mixed coloured target indicators. Within a very short space of time a large area of ground and air space became a great scene of brilliance, supplemented by searchlights and flak. It was then that I knew I had not been alone and was in good company for now I could see discipline and determination epitomised by the bomber force over the target area. For me, this impressed more than anything I had seen or taken part in during the Second World War, crews flying for many hours unseen by one another, yet to arrive over the target right on time, just as they had been instructed at the briefing.

"When home on leave, my father was keen to know all about operational flying and he quite touched me by asking if he could be my gunner. As for my mother, I said very little but there was one moment when she said: 'Your father told me that a German fighter came so close to you one night that you could read the number on it.' Now mother was known for exaggerating stories and became most indignant when I explained it would be impossible to read the number on the side of an aircraft at night. However, when father joined us she asked: 'Did you not tell me that a German fighter flew so close over the top of his cockpit he could read the number?' To this I responded 'Oh that was an FW190.' 'Yes, yes, that's the number!' came the reply from mother.

"Upon returning from an operation, a tot of rum was issued to each member of the crew, but Eddie Donahue, my bomb-aimer, who came from Montreal in Canada, knew I was teetotal and asked if he could have my ration and I was only too pleased to agree. He always had my tot but never failed to ask beforehand.

"Some years after the war, Eddie came to England and one evening my wireless operator, Jock Stewart, and flight engineer, Harry Bulman, joined us for dinner at the RAF Club in London. Later in the evening I suggested we retire to the Cowdray Bar for a last drink. I looked at Eddie and said "I know what you're going to have." He replied: "Oh yes, Clem, what is that?" I said: 'A rum!' "

After completing his tour, he had a spell at Gamston in Nottinghamshire flying Hurricanes engaged in fighter affiliation work. After a heavy landing one day, he was taken to a local RAF hospital where he was examined by an MO who warned him not to try to fly heavy aircraft, he was just too small.

He added: "He asked me what I had been doing before flying Hurricanes and I told him I'd done 36 ops on Lancasters!"

105. 625 Squadron at Scampton in June 1945. Pictured here are all members of A Flight. They include W/O E.N. Bailey, W/O Knight, Flt Lt McGrory, F/O White, P/O Slater, F/O Pollack and W/O Mitchell, a New Zealander.

The Poles at Faldingworth

IT ONLY took a year to build RAF Faldingworth — and some of the pilots who flew from there later said they could notice.

Faldingworth had something of a reputation amongst 1 Group pilots of having the worst runways in Lincolnshire. They said it was built on boggy land and it was this which caused the undulations in the main runway.

"I wouldn't even have crash landed there," one ex-1 Group pilot said. Certainly no one seemed to envy 300 Squadron when it moved in with its Wellingtons in February 1944. No one envied 300 anything at that time. They were still flying Wellingtons, albeit the final version, while everyone else in 1 Group had converted to four-engined Lancasters long ago.

But the Poles didn't mind. They were happy to be flying anything so long as it achieved their solitary aim of attacking the enemy.

Polish squadrons, be they in Fighter or Bomber Command, were amongst the most aggressive fliers in the Royal Air Force. Many had flown against the Germans first in 1939 in antiquated Polish aircraft which were brutally treated by the Luftwaffe with its then sophisticated Messerschmitts and Junkers. Some went on to fly for the French Air Force before it, too, was driven out of the sky.

So they had personal scores to settle. And the best way to settle them was to drop as many bombs as possible on the nation which had raped and ravaged their own land.

300 (Masovian) Squadron had been formed with all-Polish aircrew at Bramcote in July 1940 as part of No 6 (Training) Group. It moved to Lincolnshire almost immediately, and flew from Swinderby, just off the Lincoln-Newark road, and was quickly integrated into the newly reformed 1 Group. They converted to Wellingtons and over the next three and a half years operated mainly from Hemswell, the sturdy pre-war station near Caenby Corner, and Ingham, the strictly hostilities-only airfield between Hemswell and Scampton.

But in March 1944 they were moved for the last time, a few miles across the rich Lincolnshire farmland to Faldingworth, an airfield which was to become part of the history of the Polish Air Force in exile.

The decision to build an airfield at Faldingworth was taken back in the summer of 1941 when it seemed the whole of Lincolnshire was being planned as one vast landing ground for bombers. The site had formerly been the Toft Grange decoy and work began that August. Eleven months later such was the build-up of pressure on the RAF that Faldingworth opened, ready or not. In most cases it was a definite not. The runways were down and there were a few buildings scattered around. But it was nowhere near finished. Nevertheless the station formally opened on July 1, 1943.

106. Ground and air crew pictured at Faldingworth in the spring of 1945.

It was clearly not ready for Bomber Command and it was decided to use Faldingworth in the short term as a base for a Heavy Conversion Unit until such time as it was ready to be used by bombers. It was to be a satellite of the 1 Group HCU at Lindholme, near Doncaster, and in early August the first elements of 1667 HCU began to arrive with their mixed bag of Lancasters and Halifaxes and the first course began almost immediately, training new crews on four-engined aircraft before they were sent on to their squadrons. That first course claimed Faldingworth's first casualty of the war, a navigator who died when his aircraft was wrecked in a bad landing.

In November it was decided to concentrate all Lancaster training in 1 Group in one place and the Lancasters at Faldingworth moved out to Lindholme leaving only the Halifaxes, a rugged, sturdy aircraft which in its early marques was thoroughly detested by the new crews and the instructors alike. Thirty-two Halifaxes operated from Faldingworth for the next two months before it became a sub-station within 14 Base which formed on January 6, 1944 at RAF Ludford Magna.

By early February the Halifaxes had gone and preparations were under way for the arrival of the Poles of 300 Squadron. They were currently at Ingham and were in the process of converting from their Wellington Xs to Lancasters; the first aircraft arrived on March 1 and two days later 300 began operations initially as a one flight squadron. That first trip was a "gardening" expedition to Lorient and three Wellingtons laid mines off the French port, which was one of the primary Atlantic U-boat bases. The station's records noted that the operation marked the 50th trip for Warrant Officer A. Blachowicz.

Two weeks later the conversion to Lancasters was almost complete and 300 flew their new aircraft for the first time in a raid on Rouen. A week later they suffered their first losses, two experienced crews failing to return from a raid on Karlsruhe. "The loss of these crews presents a severe set-back for the whole squadron," noted the official record.

There were over 600 Poles at Faldingworth by now, 598 men and 61 Polish Waafs. This was in addition to 500 RAF and Waaf personnel — giving an idea of the manpower needed to run even a small bomber station.

There was another bad night for 300 on May 22. Nine aircraft were prepared for a Main Force attack on Dortmund but one aircraft suffered an engine failure soon after take-off. As the pilot tried to land, a wing tip clipped the top of the bank at the end of the firing range and the Lancaster crashed. Three of seven men on board were killed and the other four seriously injured. Of the eight which joined the attack on Dortmund, one failed to return. Four nights later another Polish crew was lost on a raid on Aachen and two more of the eight aircraft sent to Gelsenkirchen in mid-June. This particular raid coincided with the formation of a second flight at Faldingworth comprised entirely of British crews. The two crews lost were all Polish and again the station records speak of a "serious set-back" to the Polish unit.

107. Four Polish VC holders pictured at Faldingworth, 1945.

Gradually more Polish crews became available and were introduced into B Flight. But the supply of Polish airmen to make good the losses was finite and it became increasingly difficult to preserve the national identity of the squadron that summer. In the two month period from late June to the end of August 12 crews were lost, half of them Polish, almost all of whom were highly experienced airmen.

But the end of summer marked a watershed in the history of 300 Squadron. They were to lose only two more aircraft, even though by the beginning of 1944 they were able to provide up to 15 Lancasters for 1 Group operations. Among those lost was one of the squadron's most experienced pilots, Squadron Leader Knoarzewski, the A Flight commander. His Lancaster failed to return from a raid on Dortmund in February. That figure is due perhaps as much to the experience of the 300 crews as the luck which had to go with any men in Bomber Command in those days. Plenty of aircraft were damaged (two on the very last raid of the war on Berchtesgarten) and a number of men injured.

One of those was Warrant Officer Zygmunt Bednarski, a pilot typical of the men flying the 300 Squadron Lancasters at that time. He had flown with the Polish Air Force against the Germans in 1939, with the French against the Germans in 1940 and finally with the British, first as a Mosquito fighter-bomber pilot and then as a Lancaster pilot in the final months of the war. By the time of the Berchtesgarten raid he had more than 3,000 hours in his log book. There were not many Bomber Command pilots around with that amount of time in the air.

As the war ended 300, like most Bomber Command squadrons, was entrusted with Manna operations, dropping food to the starving Dutch, and with flying home PoWs. They were also given the task of ferrying supplies to the Polish Red Cross, initially in Brussels and later in Germany, a task they were to do with great relish.

300 Squadron was to remain at Faldingworth for another 18 months before the squadron was finally disbanded. Some of the Polish airmen opted to return to their own country but many remained in England.

108. A superb shot of 300 Squadron Lancasters in formation over Lincolnshire in the late spring or early summer of 1945.

The Poles were but a small part of Bomber Command and were looked upon with something approaching awe by other squadrons. Many of their pilots had previously flown fighters and they tended to fly their Lancasters in the same way. Warrant Officer Bednarski was once coned by all the searchlights over one German target but, by flying his Lancaster in the way he had once flown a Mosquito, he evaded them. It was an uncomfortable experience for his crew but they lived to tell the story back at Faldingworth. The same pilot also recalls an attack on Cleve when they came in at 18,000 feet only to be told to descend to 4,000 feet to bomb in front of advancing Allied troops. He simply put his flaps and wheels down and went down like a lift through thick cloud before he reached the required height and bombed on the target indicators.

"Quite simply, they were mad buggers," said one ex-1 Group pilot. But they were superb airmen and the qualities of the bomber men were just as evident as those of the Polish fighter pilots in the Battle of Britain.

109. ***above:*** *General Borkomorowski inspects Polish airmen at Faldingworth during a visit in 1945.*
110. ***below:*** *Polish and British aircrew at Faldingworth. The man third from the right in the flying jacket had a strong premonition of death and was killed shortly after this picture was taken.*

111. End of a veteran. A 300 Squadron Lancaster at Faldingworth after a wheels-up landing.

112. All that remains of a burnt-out 300 Squadron Lancaster. The pale finish on the visible remains would indicate this was a post-war crash.

113. The dog pictured with 300 Squadron aircrew occasionally flew on operations with the Poles at Faldingworth. One day, according to squadron legend, it was about to board an aircraft when it turned tail and bolted. That aircraft failed to return that day.

114 & 115. ***above and below:*** *Australian Prime Minister Mr John Curtin pictured at Binbrook with the CO of 460 Squadron, Group Captain Hughie Edwards VC. It was during his visit to the Australian squadron that the Premier received on behalf of the people of Australia Lancaster G-George, one of 460's veteran Lancasters. It was later flown out to Australia and is now preserved in a museum at Canberra. The second picture shows the Premier disembarking from G-George after being shown round the aircraft.*

Beating the Chop at Binbrook

WHEN IVAN Heath and his crew were posted to A Flight of 460 Squadron on June 1, 1943 they were not expected to live for more than a few weeks. The Binbrook squadron, which was to suffer among the heaviest casualties in Bomber Command, was going through its worst period for losses.

Heath survived those few weeks and went on to do something quite rare at Binbrook in those days, finish a full tour of 30 ops. Then he confounded Fate again by joining 8 Group and doing another 46 with three Pathfinder squadrons before finally being grounded.

The gunner from Nottingham had crewed up with two Englishmen and four Australians at Lichfield. Together they went through their Heavy Conversion Unit at Lindholme and were posted to Binbrook. That summer was a bad time for Bomber Command, a bad time for 460 at Binbrook. Every raid was costing one or two Lancasters. Seven were lost in one night with another ditching in the sea, a full 25 per cent of 460's strength gone in one operation.

"When we arrived it was the practice to put new crews' names at the bottom of the Flight list. Within three weeks our name was at the top of that list," said Heath.

He was to remain with 460 until October, a five month period in which he and his crew flew 30 times to Germany or Northern Italy. The night his tour ended, his skipper, Joe Munsch, said: "Right, that's it." Within 24 hours Ivan Heath had been posted away and it was 1982 before he was to meet any of his crew again.

Today he sums up his five months at Binbrook succinctly. "It was just plain frightening. We were losing one or two aircraft every time we went out. I lost a lot of friends in those months, good friends. There was one chap I had a two bob bet with to see who would survive the longest. He went after 13 trips."

It was that kind of macabre humour which kept some of them going. Heath remembers going into Grimsby with his crew and seeing girls waiting outside the Savoy Cinema for airmen he knew had been killed in the last few days. "We would tell them bluntly that their boy friend had got the chop and then ask them if they wanted to go out with us."

In his first two months at Binbrook morale was low. It was simply that crews had little hope of completing their tours. Many had become resigned to death.

"The sickness rate went up, that was always the first sign," said Heath. "You only had to sneeze and you were tempted to go to see the MO to tell him you were unfit to fly. And there was a lot of tension; we were snapping at one another all the time."

Surprisingly, he can remember only one case of an airman being declared LMF — lacking in moral fibre — during this period. The man in question was a young Scots pilot. The Lancasters took with them on every trip a photo flash flare which ignited over the target and enabled a photograph of their bombing point to be taken. This young man returned from two trips to the Ruhr with clear photographs of the Dutch coast. He was stripped of his rank and posted away in disgrace. But he survived: Heath was to meet him on a train after the war.

What really boosted morale at Binbrook was the introduction of window, the thin aluminium strips which, when scattered by the bomber stream, totally confused the German radar system. It was used, with enormous success, on the first of the Hamburg raids and losses dropped dramatically as the tiny strips effectively blinded the night-fighters (window had been available to Bomber Command for some time but its use was delayed because of fears that the Germans might copy the idea and resume an effective bombing campaign on Britain. The Germans, ironically, had developed their own version about the same time and had not used it for exactly the same purpose). Now, with window, crews believed they had at least a chance of making it to the magical 30.

Morale was also boosted during this period by visits to Binbrook by the King and by Bomber Harris himself. Harris shook hands with Heath and his crew before they left Binbrook for a raid on Milan and later watched the squadron taking off.

Some historians paint a picture of Harris as a man remote from his squadrons and whose rare visits to operational stations were solely to deliver roastings to squadrons where morale had reached rock bottom. But Ivan Heath, like many other ex-1 Group aircrew I have spoken to, disagrees with this. Harris did make only infrequent visits to his squadrons, particularly those in the north, but this was because of the sheer pressure of his job at High Wycombe. And when he did go those crews remember him as a forceful and enthusiastic supporter of what they were doing. He was, in short, a man they admired greatly.

116. A first taste of snow for Flight Sgt Jack Wilson, an Australian with 460 Squadron at Binbrook during the winter of 1944/45.

117. Even the engines of this 460 Squadron Lancaster at Binbrook carried names. The port inner was Christopher J. and the port outer was Betty. A son and daughter? The aircraft itself was O-Oboe.

Two other men Heath remembers from his days with 460 are Hughie Edwards, the 460 CO and holder of the Victoria Cross, and Air Commodore Arthur Wray, the crippled ex-RFC pilot who was Base commander at Binbrook and flew on ops as often as he could. When Wray and Edwards were not flying, they would always be at the side of the runway to see their boys off safely and they were usually there when the Lancasters returned.

On the day that Wray stepped down as Base commander he said in a message to his squadrons that his greatest regret was that he had only been allowed to do two operational flights. Yet crews from Binbrook, Kelstern and Waltham remember numerous occasions when he would turn up at dispersal in his flying kit to beg a lift to the Ruhr or Berlin. And Ivan Heath remembers, too, the times he heard Wray calling Binbrook when his aircraft was returning and a voice saying: "The one-legged chap's back!"

The one consolation Binbrook crews had was the accommodation they enjoyed in what was one of only two permanent stations then used by 1 Group. Heath and his crews actually lived in one of the married quarters, a two-bedroomed house where all seven of them slept.

He remembers the Australians as "wild" and recalls one party held on Cleethorpes Pier to celebrate the squadron's 1,000th sortie when all the fire buckets were emptied and refilled with beer and at least one Australian airman fell into the sea. So riotous were some of their parties that the Australians were in danger of being barred from Grimsby and Cleethorpes.

He recalls, too, happy nights at the Marquis of Granby in Binbrook village and the wooden hut near the camp gates where two pretty young ladies served sardine sandwiches and mugs of tea.

All this contrasted with the danger they faced every time they stepped into their Lancasters. There were few raids when Heath's aircraft did not return pock-marked by flak. After one raid one of their ground crew found a piece of shrapnel embedded in his flying helmet.

But one of his most hair-raising moments came when he was actually on the ground at Binbrook. The whole squadron had been bombed up for a raid on Cologne and he was in his turret making a few last minute checks when an aircraft parked less than 150 yards away caught fire. It was loaded with 14,000lbs of bombs and Heath knew exactly what was going to happen. So he ran

118. Lucky to be alive. The crew of AR-O, B Flight, 460 Squadron pictured at Manston in Kent in January 1945 after an emergency landing following a mid-air collision with another Lancaster en route for a raid on Munich. They are (left to right, back row): Dave Fellowes, rear gunner, D. Collett, navigator, Arthur Whitmarsh RAAF, pilot, Jack Wilson RAAF, wireless op; (front) A. Shepherd, engineer, Ken De La Mare, mid-upper gunner and Jock Turnbull, bomb-aimer.

for his life. He sheltered first in a bomb crater and finally made it to a corn field at the side of the airfield before the Lancaster and its bomb load exploded, badly damaging six other aircraft and wrecking a nearby hangar. But such was the determination among squadrons in those days that a few hours later 16 aircraft left Binbrook for a raid on Cologne.

Some members of his crew still had a few trips to do to complete their tours when Ivan Heath finally chalked up his 30th and to this day he has still not been able to trace them. He often wonders what happened in particular to the wireless operator, Bob Froggatt, who came from Burton-on-Trent and married a Cleethorpes clippie a few days after the Peenemunde raid.

Heath himself had a spell instructing after leaving Binbrook and then volunteered for Pathfinders, completing another 46 trips with 156, 405 and 35 Squadrons in 8 Group. He won the DFM for shooting down a Ju88 night-fighter "and just surviving" and admits to being bitterly disappointed when finally told he was being grounded.

"I remember watching the lads go off that night with tears in my eyes because I couldn't go with them. I had volunteered to go on to do 100 trips but there were just too many aircrew coming through by then and they thought I had had enough."

119. N. Carter and crew, 12 Squadron, April 1944. They were lost on the Mailly-le-Camp raid on May 3/4.

The Disaster at Mailly-Le-Camp

IF NUREMBURG was the greatest disaster to befall Bomber Command, then Mailly was its equivalent for 1 Group. It was supposed to be a milk-run of a raid but it was to claim 42 Lancasters and their crews, two-thirds of them from the North Lincolnshire squadrons.

On the night of May 3/4, 1944 346 Lancasters and 14 Mosquitoes from 1 and 5 Group were sent to Mailly-le-Camp, a small French village 80 miles east of Paris, between the towns of Troyes and Chalons-sur-Marne.

Close to the village was a former French army barracks and workshop area known to be in use by the German army for training and reinforcing Panzer units and believed to be the base for at least 10,000 men.

The invasion was little more than a month away and it was felt, with some justification, that a Panzer base such as Mailly so close to Normandy could pose a very serious threat to the Allied hopes.

The might of Bomber Command was now being used to prepare the way for that invasion by eliminating military and transport targets across a wide area of France and the Low Countries. Mailly was a natural target for Harris' Lancasters.

On the morning of May 3 Sir Arthur Harris decided that conditions would be just right during the coming night for the attack on Mailly-le-Camp and it was agreed it would be an all-Lincolnshire affair with the Lancasters of 1 and 5 Groups hitting the barracks on a bright, moonlit night.

Because of the barracks' proximity to the village, it was also decided that the attack would be carried out at low level with markers placed accurately and the whole raid co-ordinated by a Master Bomber. Additionally, the raid had to take place quickly before most of the German troops had time to reach the shelters and before the night-fighters arrived in what would be perfect conditions for them.

The attack was to open at midnight with aiming points at each end of the main group of barrack buildings and a third on the tank workshops. Four Mosquitoes led by Wing Commander Leonard Cheshire would place markers on the first of these and then the area would be illuminated by 5 Group's own Pathfinders, 83 and 97 Squadrons. 140 Lancasters from 5 Group would then attack.

Ten minutes later Cheshire was to mark the second aiming point which would be attacked by 140 1 Group Lancasters in the second wave. At the same time 1 Group's Binbrook Special Duties Flight was to mark the third aiming point and another 30 1 Group Lancasters would attack that target. It was a complex plan but, given the right conditions and a bit of luck, it should work.

The Lancasters began taking off soon after 10 o'clock that night. It was a short trip (raids on France were counted as only a third of an operational sortie towards the completion of a tour: that was changed after Mailly) and they crossed the French coast near Dieppe at 12,000 feet before beginning to lose height to reach Mailly at the required bombing height of 5,000 feet.

The first part of the operation went almost perfectly. Cheshire's first markers were slightly off target but a second dropped by Wing Commander Dave Shannon from just 400 feet fell in exactly the right position. The Main Force Controller, Wing Commander L.C. Deane of 83 Squadron, then called in the first wave.

While all this was going on the 5 Group Lancasters had been orbiting 15 miles north of Mailly waiting for the message to go in and bomb. But when Deane called in the first wave only a few responded. His VHF transmission was being drowned out by an American forces broadcast. A morse message proved equally useless.

A few crews made out Deane's message. Others saw Lancasters going in to bomb and used their own initiative. Their bombing was remarkably accurate, most of the five-ton loads going down exactly on the target markers.

By now Cheshire realised what was happening. He himself could not communicate with the Main Force and attempts to call in all the bombers immediately or alternatively abandon the raid went unheard. So he ordered in the final markers with the object of bringing the orbiting bombers in.

In the meantime, the 1 Group aircraft had begun arriving at the holding point and there were now more than 250 Lancasters slowly circling burning yellow Target Indicators. Night-fighters were inevitably attracted to the area likes moths to a flame.

It was soon after the first Lancaster exploded that angry voices began to be heard on the R/T channels, and most were directed at Cheshire.

The first clear orders came from the deputy controller, Wing Commander Neville Sparks from 83 Squadron. He told the crews not to bomb and to wait. But he could do little to quell the rising tide of concern among crews orbiting those burning TIs.

Some crews used their initiative and moved away from the main area; others followed orders. They were the ones who were to suffer most during the next few awful minutes.

More and more fighters were arriving. The skies seemed filled with tracer and there were burning Lancasters everywhere. But there was still no order to bomb. So bright was the moonlight that crews could identify individual fighters. It was, for those who were there, perhaps the most terrifying night they were to spend in a Lancaster.

The confusion was finally ended when Flying Officer Edwards of 97 Squadron released his markers on the second target. When Squadron Leader Sparks was satisfied they were in the right place, he ordered: "Go in and bomb." The rush that followed was later described as like being at the starting gate at the Derby.

The target area was quickly enveloped in huge explosions and fires as scores of Lancasters dropped their 4,000lb "cookies" and 500lb high explosive bombs on a clearly-marked target from just 5,000 feet.

The agony of the Lancasters was not, however, over. Some of the fighters had fuel and ammunition left and they followed the stream as it headed first for Chartres and then towards the Normandy coast north of Bayeux, ironically crossing the very landing beaches the raid was to help protect. More aircraft were shot down including that of Squadron Leader Sparks. He evaded capture and was back at Coningsby before the end of June.

One German night-fighter crew was later credited with shooting down no fewer than five Lancasters. This was not unusual. Of the large numbers of twin- and single-engined fighters sent to intercept raids, few would actually make contact and even fewer would succeed in shooting down RAF bombers. The enormous successes were due almost entirely to the skill of a relatively small number of pilots and their crews.

It was not a totally one-sided battle. Bomber crews were later to claim eight fighters downed together with two "probables". But they left behind the wreckage of 42 Lancasters, 11.6 per cent of the force dispatched that night. Of those no fewer than 28 were from the 173 sent by 1 Group, a loss rate in excess of 16 per cent.

Binbrook's 460 Squadron lost five of the 17 Lancasters it sent, almost a third of the squadron's effort that night. 101 Squadron at Ludford also lost five (the village of Ludford is now actually twinned with a French village near Mailly-le-Camp where two 101 Squadron crews lost in the raid

120. ABC-equipped Lancaster at Ludford in 1944. This may well have been one of the early batch of aircraft to be fitted with the Rose turret.

are buried). 166 at Kirmington lost three, 12 and 626 at Wickenby four and three respectively, 103 and 576 at Elsham four and three respectively and 625 Squadron at Kelstern lost three. The only operational 1 Group squadrons to escape unscathed that night were 100 at Waltham and 300 at Faldingworth.

Almost 300 aircrew had been lost. Some did survive, including Sgt Jack Worsfold of 101 Squadron. The turret of his Lancaster was shot away and, still attached to the tail section, fluttered down until it bounced off high tension cables into nearby trees.

When Worsford was captured the Germans at first refused to believe his story and maintained he was an agent dropped during the raid. Where, they demanded, was his parachute? It was only after the remains of his turret were found that his story was believed.

The results on the ground were good but not as good as Bomber Command had hoped. Reconnaissance photographs later showed that the targets themselves, and particularly the barrack blocks, had been totally destroyed. German records later showed that 218 men had been killed and 156 wounded, many of them highly-trained NCOs. In addition 65 vehicles and 37 tanks were destroyed. Hardly a fair exchange for 42 Lancasters and their crews.

The bombing had been remarkably accurate, so much so that no villagers were killed although some casualties were caused by crashing aircraft.

Back on the airfields of North Lincolnshire there was much criticism of the way the raid had been handled and most was directed at Cheshire and 5 Group. It was not justified. It was not his plan and he could hardly have been held responsible for the communications failure.

One ex-1 Group pilot told me during my research for this book: "Mailly was just a gigantic cock-up. If only we had been allowed to have gone in and bombed straight away many of those lads lost that night would have returned. As it was, I just thank God we saw what was happening and decided to steer clear of those TIs around which everyone was orbiting."

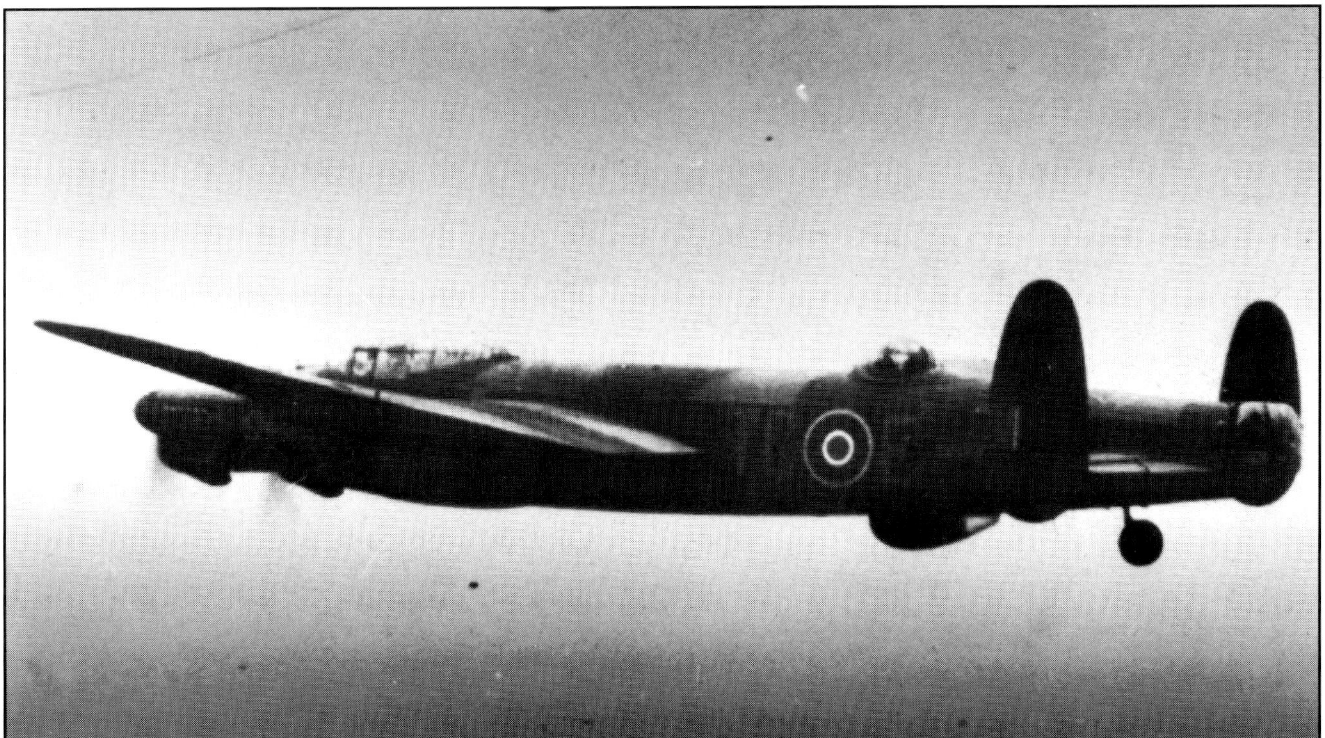

121. Lancaster Mk I NG223 TC-E2 of 170 Squadron at Hemswell pictured on ops in 1944.

122. Back at The Chopper. Ex-166 Squadron crew members pictured at a reunion outside their wartime local, the Marrowbone and Cleaver at Kirmington. They are (from the left): Jim Wright, Gordon Ballantine RNZAF, Chas Martin RNZAF, Jake Bracey and Harry Kelly.

Lonely Dispersals

The evening light was dying on that bleak November day,
When near the Wolds of Lincolnshire, I came upon the way
That led me through a hawthorn hedge to what was once my home,
For one brief, crowded hour of life — a lonely aerodrome.

The peri-track, where stately aircraft taxied round each night
Between the hooded rows of winking red and bluish light
Was overgrown; and of the runways, little could be seen,
Where once impatient kites had waited for the green.

Amid the desolation, it was hard to bring alive
The vanished erks and Lancasters of Squadron 625.
The scene had altered much with time; yet here and there a spot
Of oily, trodden earth remained, reminding me a lot
Of all the boys I served with once from Mersey, Thames and Tyne
Whose lives, no one but God knew why, had intertwined with mine.

A-Apple's old dispersal was the first to catch my eye;
And standing there I thought of Chalkey's usual DI.
He'd kick the cowlings, tap the stubs and shrouds and dip the oil,
Then disappear inside the cockpit, dodging further toil.
He'd check the fuel on the gauges, then he'd hit the hay
And sign up in the Seven Hundred later in the day.
A's Irish skipper used to grin and murmur "Holy heck!
It's only by the Grace of God I got her off the deck."

When ops were scrubbed the flight mechanics on B-Baker's crew
Stripped off in record time revealing radiant Best Blue.
And while the news was passing round the Flight from mouth to mouth
The three of them were queueing for the last bus into Louth.

C-Charlie's rigger never left the kite without his cup,
And always seemed to be the first to holler "Naafi up!"
The Naafi bint would park as near as possible to C
While bods from all directions ran and yelled for wads and tea.
Then straddle-legged on cookies, there we'd sit for ever more
Except on days when Chiefy felt particularly sore.

Across the track from Charlie stood a venerable kite,
D-Dog, affectionately called the mother of the Flight.
And tho' in flight her skipper said her port wing always rose,
She'd more than 90 bombing decorations painted on her nose.

The nicest aircraft of them all was E — she stood alone,
But perhaps my view was prejudiced: E-Easy was my own.
My oppo did the starboard motors, I DI'd the ports;
And Darkie cleaned the Perspex when he wasn't out of sorts.
The snags were always minor ones; she never sprang a leak,
Just now and then a mag-drop was the worst we had to seek.

But here's where F-Freddie stood that fateful Autumn morn,
With starboard outer shattered and fuselage all torn.
Before we'd even checked the wheels, the chaplain led the rush,
To reach the dying Wireless Op; and in the silent hush
Of that sad dawn, we seemed to leave the dying in the lurch
For just two minutes, while he had the comforts of his church.
The Ego Te Absolvo of the whispered words came clear
To where we knelt in silence with that awful presence near.
And when the padre signalled us to lift the dying W/Op
We knew that one more airman had been briefed for his last op.

G-George's pan dispersal was the easiest to find,
For that old flying oil tank left a wizard trail behind
Of blackened earth for yards around. She never missed a trip
Without returning looking just like one gigantic drip.
Both her fitters, Blondie and young Paddy, were a pair
Of philosophical blighters; they never seemed to care
How much they had to work on her. They loved old George's bones
And never could appreciate their rigger's patient groans
When George would rattle back from ops, all bathed in filthy oil.
They'd pat her props and smile, and start another hopeless toil.
Once Blondie tried to fix the leaks but Paddy said: "Ah sure!
They're nothing that a duster dipped in petrol wouldn't cure."

One rainy night poor Taffy bogged H-Harry in the mire,
Then turned her sharply to the right and pranged her starboard tyre.
He got the tractor driver and at last they pulled her out,
But not before her wing-tip from a trestle caught a clout.
Now Taffy never lived it down; yet craftily he'd sigh
When thinking of the weeks his kite lay up in R and I.

***J**-Johnny used to shed her wheels like mongrels shed their fleas,*
For Johnny had an awkward rigger difficult to please.
He'd never sign for his DI unless the tyres were sound;
And one day poor old Chiefy nearly grovelled to the ground
And wrang his hands and murmured: "If you sign, I'll take the can.
So come on Tubby, sign up now and be a decent man."
But Tubby was self-righteous, and said: "I hold the lives
Of seven boys who fly this kite, and some of them have wives."
So after that it seemed that Tubby always got his way,
But what he cost the RAF I wouldn't dare to say!

***J**ust as the dusk was gathering and night began to fall,*
I came upon the loneliest dispersal of them all.
At least it always seemed more lonely since the night
We waited there to see K-King returning from her flight.
The other kites had landed; all the aircrew bods had gone.
And tho' they said 'twas hopeless waiting, still we waited on
Till dawn broke palely through the mist. For us, it was all the same
As yet another day began. But K-King never came . . .

***T**he sad wind now was sobbing through the grasses on the verge*
Of K-King's old dispersal, like a melancholy dirge.
The empty space seemed like some anguished soul whose friends have fled,
Condemned throughout eternity to sorrow for her dead.
And so here are all the old dispersals, dull and overcast
With sombreness, while silently they mourn a noble past.
They hold the consecrated earth where Britain's happy band
Of heroes walked their last few footsteps in their native land.

***B**ut night came swiftly, and I feared the past would leave its mark*
More vividly on that deserted airfield in the dark.
I took one last look round me at the silent, ghostly Flight
then scrambled through the hawthorn hedge and vanished in the night.

*Written by **P**hilip **J**. **O'K**eefe, a Dubliner who was a member of the ground servicing crew at Kelstern with 625 Squadron during the war. He died in 1974.*

123. Sqdn Ldr John Buller, 625 Squadron Signals Leader, pictured at Kelstern with the squadron's aircrew wireless operators.

Touch Down on the Humber

EVERY SQUADRON had a rogue Lancaster. They were the equivalent of the Friday car; something was always going wrong.

At North Killingholme, the black sheep amongst 550 Squadron's Lancasters was N-Nan, a veteran aircraft which was referred to by more than one crew as "that old cow".

Its main failings were its engines and its inability to climb to a respectable height. It had a nasty habit of engine failure, particularly on ops.

Tom Elliott was a wireless operator with 550 in 1944 and his crew was allocated N-Nan for one raid when their regular aircraft, P-Peter, needed attention from their ground crew.

Sure enough, not long after take-off for a daylight raid on a V-bomb site in Northern France an engine went. But even N-Nan could fly on three engines and rather than abort — something most 1 Group crews were loathe to do because of the grilling they could expect — they continued. But soon after they had bombed it became obvious they were not going to make it back to North Killingholme and they were forced to land at an American base in East Anglia.

"When we got back to North Killingholme," said Mr Elliott, the Group Captain asked what had happened. When we told him he said, and I'll never forget it, 'Jolly good show, chaps!' "

N-Nan eventually passed to an Australian crew at North Killingholme. Returning from a raid on one moonlit night, they saw what they believed was the moon glinting off the runway at North Killingholme, lowered the wheels and gently put N-Nan down. Unfortunately, what they thought was a runway turned out to be the Humber Estuary! They couldn't inflate their dinghy but they were close to the shore and all six swam to safety, raised the alarm and transport was sent from North Killingholme for them. They arrived back at the airfield in time for their post-op meal. No one was particularly sorry to see the back of N-Nan, which Mr Elliott believes is still sitting at the bottom of the Humber. That last trip was her 94th.

Tom Elliott was a pre-war regular from Berwick-on-Tweed, a ground wireless operator who later volunteered as a wireless operator/air gunner. He eventually found himself at the Operational Training Unit at Seigford where he crewed up.

"We were all sent into a hangar and told to sort ourselves out into crews," he recalled. "I crewed up with six other sergeants but my best mate said he didn't fancy my chances at all with that lot. He told me he had joined a crew which included some very experienced officers. He was lost after 14 ops."

124. Tom Elliott (second right) with members of his crew and their ground crew at North Killingholme in 1944. Other aircrew are (from the left): Dennis Purser, Bill Watson, Denis Porter and Len Davis.

His crew arrived at North Killingholme soon after the Normandy invasion and were allocated a well-used Lancaster, P-Peter, which they found to their alarm was at dispersal number 13. But P-Peter was to stand them in good stead and they did most of their 30 operations in this aircraft.

But this was another Lancaster which had its occasional problems and after one air-test they found it wouldn't fly above 16,000 feet. And as they were due to bomb a V-weapon site from 18,000, they were allocated another aircraft. S-Sugar was brand new and had only arrived at North Killingholme that morning.

As they were taking off, S-Sugar began to swing alarmingly (most Lancasters swung on take-off, but not as much as this particular aircraft). Instead of shutting off the power and aborting, their pilot opted to carry on and just as he hauled the aircraft clear of the ground, S-Sugar decided she was having none of it, went out of control and crashed at the end of the runway. A wheel came off, an engine flew into the air and finally the Lancaster came to rest with her back broken. As the crew walked away, she burst into flames.

The remainder of their tour was largely uneventful. "We were only fired at twice, and each time it was by Lancasters," said Mr Elliott, who met and married a local girl while at North Killingholme and later settled in the Grimsby area. "A lot of Lancaster gunners, particularly tail gunners, were very trigger happy and twice we came back with bullet holes from .303s in our aircraft."

125. A Lancaster of 300 Squadron at dispersal at Faldingworth. The aircraft is wearing underwing codes so this photograph probably dates from the early spring of 1946.

A Lancaster's Story

SHE WAS big, black and just like her 7,000 or so sisters.

BQ-M2 of 550 Squadron at North Killingholme was typical of the Lancasters which served with 1 Group for the last two years of the war. She was built to do a job of work and did it wonderfully well. But once the RAF had finished with her, just 13 brief months after she was built she was discarded like a toy on Boxing Day.

She was known to all on 550 Squadron as Mike-Squared, the second M on the squadron, and she looked just like every other Lancaster. No nose art, no bomb symbols. Just the big, brick-red letters BQ-M on her fuselage.

The Lancaster was delivered to North Killingholme on October 24, 1944 and was officially struck off charge on November 23, 1945. It is believed she was scrapped very shortly afterwards.

During her brief life she was flown by at least eight 550 Squadron crews, flying a total of 37 operations, including two dropping food to the Dutch. One crew, skippered by Pilot Officer Ken Sidwell, flew operationally 25 times in her.

When the war ended the RAF was awash with Lancasters and with the advent that year of its successor, the Lincoln, there was no further use for 550's Mike-Squared once the squadron itself had been disbanded.

But the Mark I Lancaster, built by Armstrong Whitworth at Coventry as NG243, was not forgotten, particularly by the men who flew in her.

One of those was Flight Sergeant Frank Pritchard, an Australian mid-upper gunner in Flt Lt Peter Sarll's crew. Sarll himself was the commander of 550's C Flight and had flown Blenheims early in the war, surviving the attacks on the Maastricht bridges. His crew had done their conversion to Lancasters at 1662 HCU at Blyton and flew operationally from February 13, 1945 until the Manna drops in early May.

Frank Pritchard, who now lives in England, has spent some time researching the history of BQ-M2, in which his own crew flew nine times, this particular Lancaster being one of 11 different machines they flew while at North Killingholme.

The history is by no means complete and Frank, whose home is at 4 The Lawns, Benfleet, Essex, would like to hear from anyone else who has memories of this particular Lancaster.

The aircraft was given its squadron codes when it arrived at North Killingholme on the morning of October 24, 1944 fresh from its Coventry builders.

After an intensive testing period, during which it was flown by Flying Officer L. Cameron DFC and his crew on cross-country and fighter affiliation exercises, the new aircraft was allocated to Flying Officer Marriott and his crew for a daylight raid on Gelsenkirchen on November 6, 1944. She was one of 738 Lancasters, Halifaxes and Mosquitoes which carried out an attack on the Nordstern synthetic oil plant and the town itself. The raid passed uneventfully for North Killingholme's debutante and she returned to base after a trip lasting five hours and 50 minutes.

Three days later Mike-Squared was on ops again, this time in the hands of Flying Officer Ken Sidwell, when the target was the refinery at Wanne-Eickel in the Ruhr. It was a five hours 40 minutes night raid, which again appears to have been without incident.

Two nights later Sidwell took Mike-Squared to the Ruhr again when the target this time was the Hoesch Benzin synthetic oil plant on the outskirts of Dortmund. Her third raid was on Duren on November 16 when 1, 5 and 8 Groups provided support for the advancing Americans.

Then it was back to Wanne-Eickel for a second raid on the oil plant. The Bomber Command War Diaries point out that on this occasion the Hannibal coal mine was destroyed. When Mike-Squared returned North Killingholme was fog-bound and she diverted to the FIDO-equipped airfield at Witchford. It had been a five hours 55 minute trip, her longest yet. The following day Sidwell flew the Lancaster on the short 35 minute hop back to North Killingholme.

Bomber Command had now reached the peak of its power and there were few days and even fewer nights when the Lancasters and Halifaxes were not ranging far and wide across Europe. 550 was next in action on November 21 when 274 1 and 8 Group Lancasters hit the marshalling yards and rail lines at Aschaffenburg. The yards themselves were badly hit but the through lines were not cut, many of the bombs falling on the town itself. This was a six hour 25 minute trip and was followed by a six-day stand-down by most of 1 Group.

It is worth noting that no bomb symbols were painted on the sides of Mike-Squared. And the same went for several other Lancasters in 550 Squadron. The feeling was among many of the squadron's crews that it was not prudent to advertise the number of raids on their Lancasters in case they were shot down.

"The last thing you wanted was the wreckage of a Lancaster with 90 trips painted on the side when there was a lynch mob around pointing to the number of times you had dropped bombs on them," said Frank Pritchard. "It was much better to let them think it was your first time out."

Mike-Squared was back in action again on the night of November 27 with a seven hour 15 minute trip to Freiburg, right on the Swiss border. It was a virgin target which intelligence believed was packed with German troops preparing to counter-attack American and French forces advancing nearby. In the event, almost 3,000 people died in the raid, few of them soldiers.

The Lancaster was taken by a third crew for her next raid, on Dortmund, on November 29 when Flying Officer Thompson was the skipper. Thompson was an Australian and had four of his fellow countrymen in his crew.

Her next raid was again in the hands of a different crew when Flying Officer Luder, another Australian, took her to Karlsruhe. Two nights later she carried yet another crew, this time skippered by Flt Lt Edlund, for a raid on the Leuna refinery, near Merseburg.

Ken Sidwell was back in the pilot's seat on her next raid six nights later when Bomber Command staged its last major night raid of the war on the pile of rubble which had once been the city of Essen. It was a highly accurate raid and the six hour trip was the first of 16 consecutive ops flown in Mike-Squared by Sidwell and his crew.

They were out again the following night when the target was the I.G. Farben factories in and around Ludwigshafen, a round trip from North Killingholme of six hours and 25 minutes. Four nights later Ulm and its lorry plants and army barracks were bombed during another lengthy raid which lasted seven and a half hours.

Mike-Squared did not fly operationally again until Boxing Day when she was among 294 Lancasters and Halifaxes which took advantage of a break in the weather to bomb St Vith, hitting German troop concentrations during the Battle of the Bulge in the Ardennes. This was BQ-M2's shortest trip so far, lasting just four hours and 23 minutes from take-off to landing.

126. This was 550 Squadron's Mike-Squared, pictured at North Killingholme in mid-March 1943 by Jack Allen, the man who had been her flight engineer for 25 of her operational sorties.

The following day 550 hit the marshalling yards at Rheydt, from where supplies were being moved up to the ground forces in the Ardennes. This turned out to be a lengthy trip for, when the squadron returned, they found North Killingholme again fog-bound and were diverted to a variety of airfields, Mike-Squared ending up at Finningley.

The Lancaster was in action again on the night of December 29 with a five hour 50 minute trip to Schloven where the refinery was bombed on Oboe through thick cloud.

Severe weather in January kept most of 1 Group aircraft grounded and 550 was only able to operate from North Killingholme infrequently and then only after Herculean efforts to clear snow and de-ice aircraft. Ken Sidwell flew Mike-Squared operationally on the 5th and 22nd of January with the only other recorded flight of the Lancaster on the 27th when Sidwell flew a three hour 25 minute cross country and bombing exercise.

It was on February 1 when Mike-Squared came perhaps the closest to joining the thousands of Lancasters which would not see the end of the war. Sidwell was just easing her off the main runway for a raid on Ludwigshafen when the port inner engine caught fire.

Flight engineer Jack Allen explained: "A conrod had come through the side of the engine, there was a bit of a fire and fuel was blowing back onto the exhaust stubs.

"I was standing at the side of the skipper and I just kept my eyes on the dials. The boost was going up, down, up again and finally it started to go altogether so I pushed the feather button.

"Our skipper did really well. We were down to about 400 feet over Habrough Station and the port wing dropped like a dose of salts. We were full of fuel and bombs and we almost went in near the station. If we had I think we would have ended up in Grimsby in bits but the skipper kept us in the area."

127. Peter Sarll (centre, rear) and his crew who flew Mike-Squared. They are (back row, from the left): Russ Longmire, navigator, Jock Murray, engineer, Peter Sarll, the pilot, Alf Coomes, wireless operator, John Seppelt, bomb-aimer; (front) Peter Robertson, rear gunner, Frank Pritchard, mid-upper gunner.

128. ***above:*** *F/O Bob Tapsell and crew, 550 Squadron, North Killingholme.*
129. ***below:*** *A Christmas party in the Sergeants' Mess at Faldingworth in 1944.*

They were ordered to take their bombs out to sea and dump them in a designated drop area before returning to North Killingholme. They were an experienced crew, otherwise they might have been sent to the diversion airfield at Woodbridge with its extra-long runway.

Jack Allen went on: "We only dropped the cookie and decided to take the rest back with us. The skipper put the Lancaster down like a duck landing on water. It was very impressive."

The following night Mike-Squared, the Lancaster which could have been reduced to strips of metal on the side of a huge crater, was back on ops. A new engine fitted, she made a six hour 40 minute round trip to Wiesbaden on the Rhine.

It was Sidwell and his crew who took BQ-M2 to Cleve on February 7 where they bombed from 500 feet to support British troops who were attempting to take the town. The following night Mike-Squared made her longest trip so far of the war with a raid along with 474 other Lancasters and Mosquitoes of 1, 5 and 8 Groups on the synthetic oil plant at Politz. It was a round trip of eight hours and 20 minutes.

Dortmund and Duisburg followed on February 20 and 21 with another long trip (seven hours 50 minutes) to Pforzeim on the 24th. Sidwell took her to Mannheim on March 1 and Cologne the following day where Mike-Squared suffered minor flak damage.

Three nights later she had a new crew on board and a new sound in the cockpit. Flt Lt Peter Sarll was the commanding officer of C Flight and a very experienced airman. He was noted for the hunting horn he always carried on ops and would sound as the aircraft was going in on a target and again as it was leaving. At first this proved to be somewhat disconcerting for his crew, five of whom were Australians and had not come across this particular form of British eccentricity before.

Sarll took Mike-Squared (and presumably his hunting horn) to Dessau on March 7. The following day Pilot Officer Alan Elliott and his crew "borrowed" Mike-Squared for the first of two cross country exercises they were to fly in what had become a reliable and dependable Lancaster.

There were two more trips in the Lancaster for Sidwell and his crew, who were fast approaching the end of their tour. Their final raid was on Paderborn on March 27. With their tour over, the crew were scattered, Sidwell going to a Heavy Conversion Unit. Within a few weeks he took a new crew out over the North Sea and their Lancaster was not seen again.

On April 9 Mike-Squared went to Kiel to take part in the bombing of the battleship Admiral Scheer and the heavy cruisers Emden and Admiral Hipper. Alongside Peter Sarll on that trip was Flying Officer J.A. Sweeney, a Canadian who was flying as second dickie.

A raid on the railway yards at Plauen followed on the 10th and her next recorded raid was 12 days later when a major raid on Bremen in support of the attack by British ground forces was

130. Elsham Waaf Margaret Dell with the crew of a Lancaster in which she flew at the end of the war.

planned. Cloud, smoke and dust quickly obscured most of the target area and the Master Bomber called the raid off before any 1 Group aircraft could attack and they were ordered home with their bombs.

On April 25 Peter Sarll took Mike-Squared on her last offensive mission of her short career when 550 took part in the raid on the SS barracks at Berchtesgarten. He made sure it was a fitting finale with three runs over the target area before being satisfied that the right target had been selected. Mike-Squared touched down at North Killingholme eight hours and five minutes after she took off.

After being recalled from a repatriation flight, BQ-M2 made her two final wartime sorties to Rotterdam as part of Operation Manna, dropping supplies of food to Dutch civilians.

And that was it as far as BQ-M2 was concerned. After the war ended and it became clear that the war in the Far East would be resolved without the use of Bomber Command she spent the remainder of her time at North Killingholme flying the occasional cross country or bombing exercise before she was finally struck off charge and flown to a maintenance unit where she was broken up.

*The crews who flew in Mike-Squared and who have been traced by Frank Pritchard were as follows:

F/O R.A. Marriott, pilot, P/O E.W. Turnbull, engineer, F/O R.W. Pratt, RCAF, navigator, F/O J. Winning, RCAF, bomb-aimer, F/Sgt Proudfoot, RCAF, rear gunner.

F/O C. George, pilot, Sgt E. Okines, engineer, Sgt J. Johnson, navigator, Sgt C. Stocker, bomb-aimer, F/Sgt T. Jeffs, wireless operator, Sgt E.W. Kilby, mid-upper gunner, Sgt Challower, rear gunner.

F/O K. Sidwell, pilot, Jack Allen, engineer, Jock Hewitt, navigator, Jack Banks, RCAF, bomb-aimer, John Chapman, wireless operator, Frank Woodley, mid-upper gunner, Dennis Whitmarsh, rear gunner.

F/O S. Thompson, RAAF, pilot, Sgt R. Wilson, engineer, F/O S. Thorp, navigator, F/O Campbell, RAAF, wireless operator, F/Sgt W. Cranfield, mid-upper gunner, F/Sgt K. Haubb, RAAF, rear gunner.

F/O E. Luder, RAAF, pilot, Sgt E. Bowman, engineer, F/O E. Jones, RCAF, navigator, Flt Lt J. Ward, bomb-aimer, F/Sgt D. McDonnell, RAAF, wireless operator, Sgt R. Furness, mid-upper gunner, F/Sgt H. Jordan, rear gunner.

Flt Lt C.J. Edlund, pilot, Sgt S. Lipfriend, engineer, F/O W. Dawson, RCAF, navigator, F/Sgt P. Barber, bomb-aimer, W/O J. Gordon, wireless operator, Sgt H. Cleghorn, mid-upper gunner, Sgt J. Carruthers, rear gunner.

P/O Alan Elliott, pilot, V.B. Gassapi, engineer, Neville Lund, navigator, Reg Francis, bomb-aimer, Dennis Scully, wireless operator, Alan Cassidy, mid-upper gunner, Bob Craig, rear gunner.

Flt Lt Peter Sarll, pilot, Sgt J. Murray, engineer, P/O R. Longmire, RAAF, navigator, F/O J. Seppelt, RAAF, bomb-aimer, F/O A. Coomes, RAAF, wireless operator, F/Sgt F. Pritchard, RAAF, mid-upper gunner, F/Sgt P. Robertson, RAAF, rear gunner.

*131. **above:** This was 550 Squadron's Q-Queenie after a tangle with a German night-fighter during a raid on Stuttgart on March 1, 1944. The fighter is believed to have attacked the Lancaster using its upward-firing cannon and it was only the superb teamwork of the crew and the skill of the pilot, Squadron Leader Hugh Grant-Dalton, which allowed them to escape.*
*132. **below:** A cheery smile from a member of the Elsham transport section.*

PM

PM

These were the men who flew and serviced D-Dog at Elsham Wolds during the winter of 1943 and spring of 1944. The crew were together during the worst period of the war for Bomber Command and their tour saw them fly to Berlin no fewer than 10 times.
Norman Storey, who was D-Dog's rear gunner, remembers the time when a South American whose son had been killed flying with Bomber Command decided to donate six gold watches to be presented to the pilots who had flown the most operational raids on Berlin. D-Dog's pilot, Flying Officer Len Young DFC, received one of those watches.
133. ***above:*** *shows the original crew at Elsham during their tour. They are (from the left, front): Paul Hawthorn, mid-upper gunner, Norman Storey, Len Young, Ron Gardner, wireless operator, Alfred Shields, navigator; (front) George Hathaway, bomb-aimer and Bill Benstead, flight engineer.*
134. ***top left:*** *A photograph which will strike a chord with every ex-Lancaster pilot, Len Young at the controls of D-Dog.*
135. ***centre left:*** *One of the ground crew had a daughter named Kath and always chalked her name on the 4,000lb cookie D-Dog carried on most raids over Germany.*
136. ***bottom left:*** *Some of the crew with their aircraft.*

LEADER

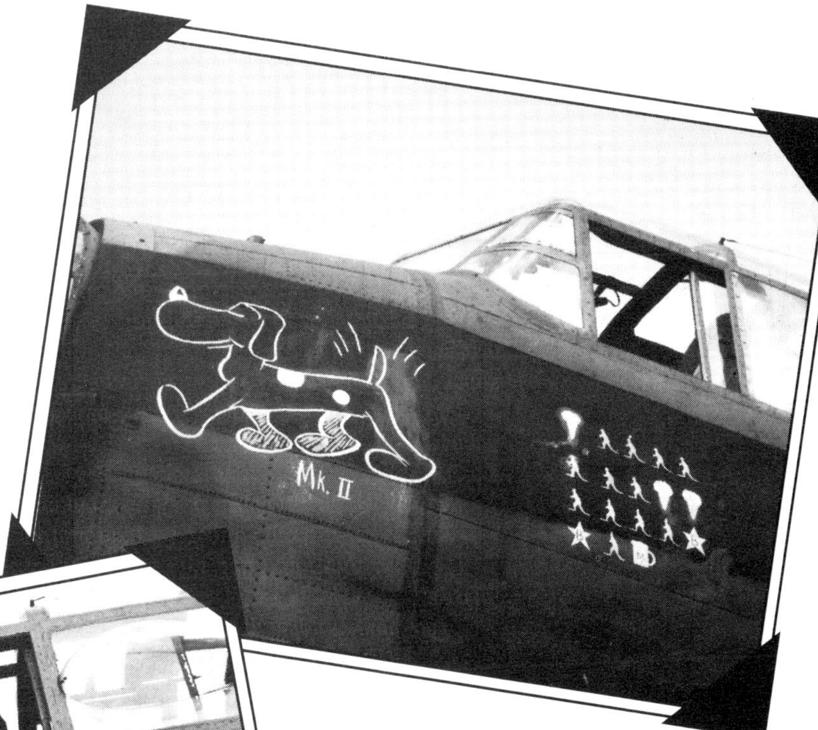

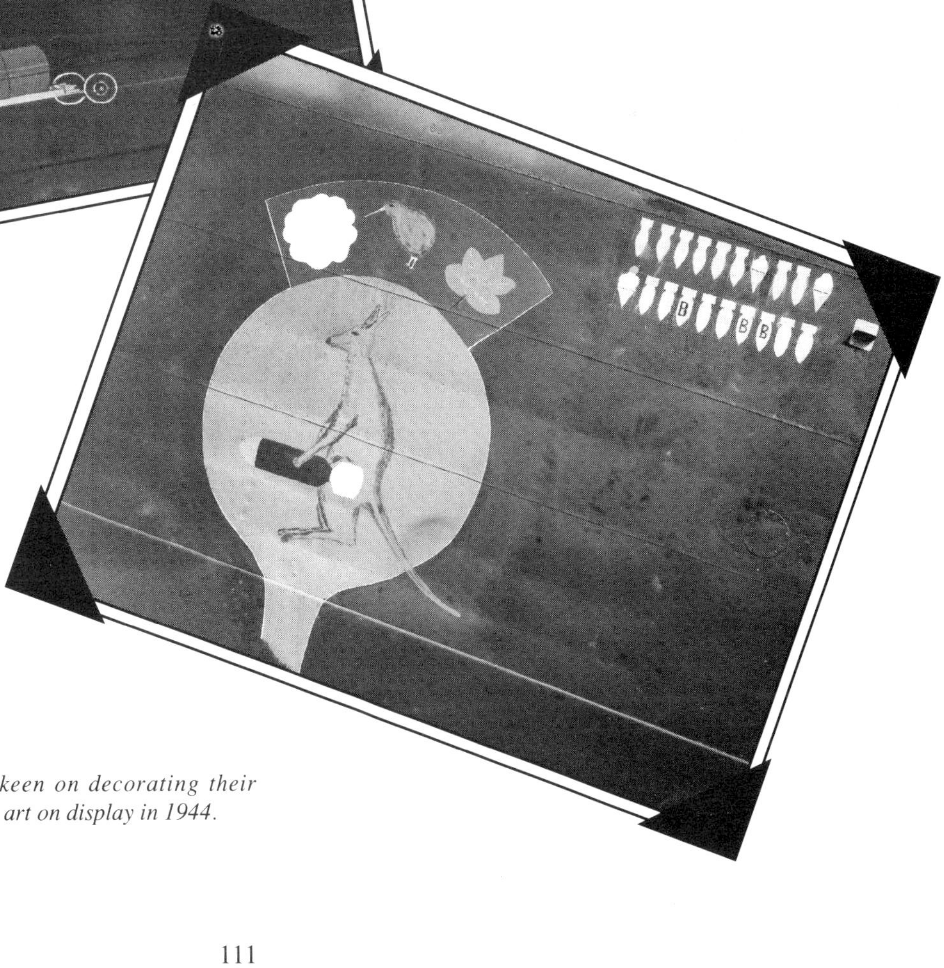

137-143. The Binbrook Aussies were keen on decorating their Lancasters. This is a selection of the nose art on display in 1944.

The Other Battle

IN OCTOBER 1943 the station medical staff at Blyton, the home of 1662 HCU, faced a new problem in trying to keep as many men flying as possible — VD.

There was usually a case or two on most airfields but that month four airmen reported sick at Blyton. It was evidently a serious problem . . .

Through some vigorous questioning, it seemed that all the cases emanated from one source, a certain lady then living in Scunthorpe.

So, on the suggestion of the station medical officer, Scunthorpe was placed out of bounds to all aircrew. "If our surmise is correct," wrote the MO in his monthly report, "a remarkable fall in VD cases will be the result."

He was right. The following month only one new case was detected and that was most certainly not the result of a liaison in Scunthorpe.

However, in December cases started to increase again, and by February were growing at a considerable rate.

It was then discovered that the lady concerned, on hearing of the ban on young men visiting Scunthorpe, had simply taken the bus to Gainsborough and had been able to pass on her affection, and infliction, to a whole new batch of men at the HCU!

144. A rare shot of 550's Phantom of the Ruhr, its longest-serving Lancaster, pictured being bombed up at North Killingholme. A total of 95 operations are logged which suggests the picture was taken in the autumn of 1944. The Phantom, which had started life with 100 Squadron at Waltham, went on to complete 121 operations. Interestingly there were some crews who refused to have ops logged on the side of their aircraft in case of reprisals if they were shot down. It is also worth noting that the Phantom's trips are recorded in rows of 13. Obviously her crews were not superstitious!

Village Inn at Binbrook

THE ROSE turret wasn't the only innovation which came 1 Group's way in 1944. Another was Village Inn, which was aimed at giving aircraft early warning of approaching aircraft.

It was operated by two infra-red beams mounted in the nose of the Lancaster, angled outwards from the aircraft. If any metal object entered the area covered by the beam it set off a series of warning pips which got louder as the target aircraft came nearer.

That was fine in practice but when Lancasters were operating in bomber streams at night, they sometimes were very close to other aircraft and Village Inn became more of a hindrance than a help.

Probably the first 1 Group squadron to receive the new equipment was 460 at Binbrook.

One crew was selected for training at the Bomber Development Unit at Newmarket and that was a new crew to the squadron, captained by Flt Sgt Jarratt. The flight engineer, John Andrew, remembers they were one of two crews trained at that time at Newmarket. The second, from 3 Group, were lost when their dinghy accidentally inflated in flight and wrapped itself round the tail, causing the aircraft to go down out of control.

Back at Binbrook, they were prohibited from flying operationally until they had trained the squadron's other crews in the use of Village Inn.

Another ex-Binbrook aircrew member who recalls Village Inn is George Toombs. "The pips sounded like sonar, but when you were in a bomber stream with lots of other aircraft nearby it used to get on our nerves," he said.

"It was activated by two lights mounted in the nose covered with an infra-red covering. We were on ops one night in very bad weather, heavy rain and the like, and this covering started peeling off. It was amazing, you could see all these aircraft flying along with what looked like car headlights on!"

That persuaded the pilots to switch off their Village Inn straight away.

145. Flying Officer Arthur Whitmarsh DFC, pictured in the veteran O-Oboe of 460 Squadron during the winter of 1944/45.

146. The catering staff in the Sergeant's Mess at Elsham.

All Those Lovely Lads

VIOLET LAIT was a South Killingholme girl who was to find work and friendship on the new airfield that was being built just off Top Road on the way to North Killingholme.

Violet then lived in Mayfield Avenue in the village and when work began on the airfield was taken on by the main contractors, Higgs and Hill, and eventually found herself driving lorries. Later, when the airfield was finished, she worked as a civilian Air Ministry employee driving trucks for the maintenance contractors on the airfield.

Violet, now Mrs Violet Simpson, still lives in South Killingholme and has many fond memories, and a few sad ones, of the brief period when the airfield was operational.

"It was a lovely time," she recalled. "They were such lovely lads on the airfield. Always full of fun and it was a fascinating place to be in the short time they were all here."

She had a boy friend among the aircrew. His name was Jeff Jefferson and she used to take him and his entire crew home with her to enjoy a roaring fire, a home-cooked meal and a pot of home-brewed tea.

One day Jeff and his happy, laughing friends were there. The next they had gone, their dispersal empty until a replacement aircraft was flown in. They were posted as missing in action.

"I didn't find out for a long time what had happened but I wrote to his mum down south for a long time. And then after the war one of the crew came back to South Killingholme to see me. He told me they had been shot down and he was the only one to get out and was made a prisoner. The rest, including Jeff, had been killed."

The offices from which she worked were close to the briefing room at North Killingholme and she would often watch as the crews filed in and saw them again as they came out. Some evenings she would watch as the aircraft flew out and the next morning would look anxiously around the dispersals to see how many had returned.

But there were happy times; the dances in the Old School, the friendliness of the young airmen, the riotous party at the Cross Keys on VJ night when the road outside was a sea of airmen who refused to let her pass in her lorry until she had promised to come back for a drink.

She also remembers the nights when she had to ferry workmen to Habrough Station to catch the train into Grimsby and the young airmen who would cadge lifts to get into town to see their wives who had moved into lodgings.

"Looking back, we had some wonderful times. There were the sad days as well but somehow they just made us want to enjoy ourselves even more."

The Cross Keys is remembered by many other airmen who were stationed at North Killingholme. It was the first pub Ted Stones, then a 19-year-old engine fitter, ever went in. That first occasion was to help the skipper of the aircraft he worked on celebrate the end of his tour of 30 ops. It was a terrific party, the highlight of which was a 550 tradition, the pilot filling his hat with beer and passing it round the assembled gathering.

Mr Stones recalls the landlord, a man named Hodson, as a crusty character who kept pigs. One night for a joke the pigs were let out by some of the high-spirited young fliers. Hodson didn't see the funny side of it and threatened dire consequences if he ever discovered who had done it.

He was also a man who liked his drink and called time every night by shouting: "Come lads and lasses, finish up your glasses; if you can't finish it, then I can!"

Ted Stones, a Portsmouth man who now lives in Humberston, recalled Station Warrant Officer Yardley, nicknamed "Lavender" for obvious reasons, as something of a martinet.

"To tell you the truth, he was a real sod. There was this path running through a particularly muddy area to the Naafi. It wasn't wide enough so he decided to have it widened and it became known as the Burma Road. It was built solely on fatigues. He had a big Irish sergeant who went around with him and they used to stand outside the airmen's mess. Anyone who came out without his hat on correctly or a button out of place was on fatigues that night, and that meant helping build his Burma Road."

He treated aircrew in exactly the same way. But one night they got their revenge. Yardley went everywhere on a bicycle. That night a group of airmen were waiting for him and he emerged sometime later from a nearby ditch, muddied and chastened.

147. ***right:*** *Waafs at Wickenby during the winter of 1944.*
148. ***below:*** *M-Mother with air and ground crew, 100 Squadron, Waltham*

Driving the Yellow Peril

THE UNSUNG heroes on most RAF camps during the war were the Waafs. They were the clerks, the parachute packers, sometimes the mechanics and as often as not the drivers who kept the station running soothly.

The "Waaferies" were always a discreet distance from the rest of the camp and were distinguishable by a few touches of home comforts here and there, a vase of flowers, perhaps a cheerful pair of curtains.

Marjorie Grey remembers the Waafery at Waltham with some affection. It was a collection of Nissen huts clustered in the lee of the village windmill, a pleasant place to be even in those days.

Mrs Grey, then Marjorie Markham, was posted to 100 Squadron as a driver in February 1943. In those days the Waafs drove anything and everything. One day it would be the coal lorry, the next the squadron dustcart. Then they might be driving the crew buses if they were on night shifts.

That would always remain one of the most memorable jobs, driving the tense young men out to their aircraft and picking them up a few hours later when their relief at returning was all too apparent.

Sometimes they would have to drive the ambulances, a job which could be distressing when they had to go out to aircraft which had brought dead or wounded crew members back from raids.

And then there was the Yellow Peril, the emergency landing vehicle which was sent out to shepherd any "foreign" aircraft which had landed at Waltham.

Later they were issued with small Hillman vans and and it was in one of these that Marjorie was to be appointed as the driver to Sqdn Ldr Bill Irvine, A Flight's commander.

Mrs Grey was to serve on a number of stations during the war but regards the 18 months she was with 100 Squadron as the highlight of her time in the Waafs. "Everyone in Waltham was so nice to us," she said. "It was a great station and I can never remember feeling unhappy there."

Like everywhere else, they had to endure the rigours of winter, but when there was sufficient fuel available conditions could be made tolerable. "Whoever was first back into the hut at night had the job of getting the stove in the middle going. Providing you had a bit of coal to get it started and coke to keep it going, you would be surprised how warm we could get that Nissen hut."

There was the regular bus service into Grimsby, the pleasant walks around Waltham, the Tea Gardens, the Ship at Barnoldby a short bike ride away.

Mrs Grey's home was only 15 miles away at East Halton (almost overlooking her final Lincolnshire posting at North Killingholme) but she spent as much time at Waltham as possible. "It was a very good place to be," she said.

The Lucky Ones

THIS WAS the crew of Pilot Officer Gordon Smart, pictured at North Killingholme in the early spring of 1945. They were among the lucky ones. By the time they arrived at an operational station losses had fallen to an almost negligible rate. The war was clearly almost over. The crew had come together at 12 OTU at Edgehill and did their heavy conversion on Lancasters at Sandtoft before joining 550 in early March. There was still time for 12 operations before the war did finally come to an end, the last two being Manna food drops over Holland, trips which counted as operational sorties because there were still pockets of German resistance in Holland. The one hatless member of the crew is Sgt Alan Rose, the rear gunner on the eight different Lancasters they were to fly on those 12 flights. He was from Kent but during his stay in North Lincolnshire met a Grimsby girl and married. They were to return to the area in the 1970s and he worked at an oil refinery built overlooking his old airfield until his death.

149. Gordon Smart's crew at Killingholme.

Dangerous Days - and Nights - at Waltham

GEORGE BRADBURY had a strange war. It started for him as a bomb-aimer with 100 Squadron at Waltham, from where he went on to be an RAF fireman at Hemswell, and he finished as a quartermaster sergeant in the 1st Northamptonshire Regiment fighting the Japanese in Burma.

But he has no doubts which was the most dangerous — his short spell at Waltham where he did five ops against German targets during 1943.

He had been trained in the United States and Canada, initially as a pilot and then on the navigator/bomb-aimer training scheme. But all this training was to be wasted after a disagreement with a wing commander at Waltham. That led to him being court-martialled for insubordination, stripped of his rank of flight sergeant and posted to Hemswell where he spent some time with the station fire service.

"I had done five ops with my crew when I had trouble with my ears. It was the cold which had got to them and on one occasion I found I could not hear properly things that were being said over the intercom. I had to get up from my position and go to talk to the wireless operator," said Mr Bradbury, who lives in Oldham.

"First of all the MO said I was unfit to fly. But this was at the time when we were short of crews and the next thing I knew was that I was told I had to fly. I frankly thought it was dangerous for a crew to have a bomb-aimer who could hear very little and I said so, probably a bit too strongly. This all led to a confrontation with this wing commander and I found myself stripped of my rank."

When he arrived at Hemswell the airfield was closed operationally while concrete runways were being laid and he found himself amongst a group of men who were looking for a safe occupation to see out the war.

He later had the opportunity to join the Army and took it, eventually finding himself fighting in the Burmese jungle. But he always looked back on his days at Waltham as the most dangerous time of his war. "While I was there 100 Squadron was beginning to lose a lot of crews. My own crew made it through to the end of their tour but there were plenty who didn't."

150. A typical dispersed accommodation site at a 1 Group airfield. This particular picture was taken at Kelstern, the Nissens seemingly arranged in a haphazard fashion in a slight dip in the Wolds, which wouldn't have helped the drainage too much.

He remembers Waltham for the direction of the main runway. Most followed the direction of the prevailing south-west to north-east wind. But Waltham's didn't. "I think it must have had something to do with the different winds over the Humber," he said. "And at one end, on the approach, there was this Royal Naval wireless station with great big masts sticking up. Sometimes you couldn't see them until right at the last minute."

He remembers an American pilot, Tommy Morgan, who had just completed his tour with 100. The rule was on taking off to climb to 2,000 feet before doing anything else. Morgan decided to do a steep climbing turn out of Waltham in his Lancaster, and collided with a Spitfire. There were no survivors.

Bradbury had done his initial bomb-aimer's training at Whitchurch on Whitleys and remembers all too well the night he bombed the town by mistake. His aircraft was approaching the bombing range near the town when George accidentally caught the bomb release button and sent a 4lb flash bomb down close to the people leaving a late evening cinema show. This was one night at the pictures they certainly would remember.

151. F/Sgt Bob Bowden, pictured on his first tour at Waltham with 100 Squadron in 1943.

Battle of the Buzz Bombs

BOMBER COMMAND'S summer campaign against German V1 sites in Northern France probably helped save the lives of thousands of people in Southern England.

The V1 was never a serious threat to the success of the invasion, but it came as a very nasty shock to people in the London area who thought the invasion would herald an end to the threat of air raids, the blackouts and everything that reminded them of the blitz three and a half years earlier.

Shortly after the Allies went ashore in Normandy the V1s began droning their way over Southern England. Many were intercepted and brought down, others went astray and crashed in the sea or at their launch sites, but many more got through and brought death and destruction to thousands of people, particularly in the London area and, sometime later, in East Anglia.

It was hoped the sites, most of which were in the Pas de Calais, would be quickly overrun by the invading British and American ground forces but their advance was to be delayed for two months. So it was left to the air forces to do what they could to remove the threat from the "buzz-bombs", the "doodlebugs" which brought a new form of terror to an already war-weary England.

That summer the full weight of Bomber Command, together with the fighter bombers of the 2nd Tactical Air Force, were launched against the ski-sites from where the bombs were launched. Most of these were spotted by reconnaissance aircraft and within hours Lancasters and Halifaxes would begin raining high explosive bombs on the sites.

During that summer Bomber Command carried out a total of 176 attacks on launch sites or V1 storage dumps in Northern France. The attacks only ended when Allied troops finally occupied the launch zones. They cost Bomber Command a total 114 aircraft, 88 Lancasters, 22 Halifaxes and four Mosquitoes.

The very last of those aircraft was from 550 Squadron at North Killingholme, E-Easy. It was one of a small number of 1 Group aircraft which took part in a concerted attack on 12 sites that day. 550's target was the Wemaers/Cappel site near Amiens.

It was the 30th and final operation for the crew of E-Easy and should have been a milk-run — a

152. This was the crew of the last Lancaster to be lost by Bomber Command in raids on the V1 sites. They are pictured at the No 1 Lancaster Finishing School at Hemswell, a rarity in itself as crews were only there for usually less than a fortnight before they went on to their squadrons. On the picture are (back row, left to right): F/Sgt E. McQuarrie RCAF, P/O S. Beeson, Sgt H. Picton, F/Sgt D. Neal; (front) Sgt Hewlett, Sgt J. Norgate and Sgt J. Trayhorn.

comfortable way to finish a tour. The aircraft was on its way back to England when it was caught by a radar-predicted flak battery near Dunkirk. E-Easy received a direct hit and went down in flames. Four members of the crew, the pilot, Pilot Officer Stanley Beeson, the navigator, Sqdn Ldr K. MacAleavey, bomb-aimer, Sgt Derrick Neal, and engineer, Sgt "Red" Hewlett, all escaped by parachute and became prisoners of war. But the wireless operator, Sgt Kenny Norgate, and both gunners, Sgts Horace Picton and Jimmy Trayhorn, were killed. All three are buried in a communal grave at Bollezeele, close to the spot where their aircraft crashed.

Sqdn Ldr MacAleavey was commander of 550's A Flight and he took over from their regular navigator, Flying Officer Cameron, for this particular trip. It was quite common on some squadrons for senior officers to accompany crews on their 30th and final trip. Cameron had joined the crew in time for their 20th operation after their first navigator, Sgt Earl McQuarrie, a Canadian, had been invalided out.

McQuarrie was the oldest member of the crew and had been a miner in Canada. He was a heavy smoker and drinker and this may have contributed to the illness which eventually led to him being admitted to Rauceby Hospital, near Sleaford, and his return later to Canada, where he died. McQuarrie had a habit of disappearing when he had had a few drinks and often when the crew left North Killingholme's "local", the Cross Keys in neighbouring South Killingholme, they found he had climbed one of the large trees outside the front door.

The crew had trained initially on Halifaxes at 1662 Heavy Conversion Unit at Blyton and, after a brief spell with 1667 HCU at Sandtoft, were posted to the No 1 Lancaster Finishing School at Hemswell and, after their three days training there, to 550 at North Killingholme. They had first flown operationally together on D-Day.

Theatre Royal,
Wickenby.

Christmas Day & Boxing Day,
at 19.00 hrs.

By kind permission of
Group Captain P. HAYNES, D.F.C.,
PRESIDENT SERVICES INSTITUTE
presents

"CINDERELLA"

An Original Adaptation of everybody's Favourite Pantomine. Specially written for the urk by the urk, to remind you of your delightful stay at hospitable WICKENBY.

ADMISSION—Officers 1/- ; S.N.C.O.'s 9d.;
W.A.A.F. and Airmen 3d.

Programme 1d. each.

THIS WAS the programme produced for the Christmas performances of Cinderella at Wickenby.

It comes from the collection of Emily Warwick, a Waaf in the station headquarters during the latter part of the war.

The panto itself was produced by Tom Turnbull, directed by Don Loker and compered by Cyril Fieldsend.

Cinderella was played by Kath Armstrong while Don Loker took time off from directing to play Prince Charming. Other members of the cast included "Smallpox" Chadburn, Taff Samuel, "Shag" Marshall, Eric Savage, Kay Collier, "Shakespeare" Arrowsmith, Vera Wade, Evelyn Darl, George Armstrong, "Wendell" Wilkie, Len Paton and Ike Cohen.

The orchestra was directed by Les Armstrong and Reg Damon was the pianist.

Just Another Raid

THOSE WHO have condemned the policies and operations of Bomber Command, particularly in the later stages of the war, have just one argument when taken to task — Dresden.

This ancient city in Saxony was levelled in a series of raids during February 13 and 14, 1945 by the Royal Air Force and, to a lesser extent, the United States Army Air Force.

The Dresden raids perhaps represented the ultimate achieved in sheer destructive might by the Allied air forces during the Second World War. The raids themselves came in three separate and quite distinct waves. First 167 Lancasters from 5 Group bombed the city. They were followed three hours later by 529 Lancasters from 1, 3, 6 and 8 Groups and, the following day, by 311 USAAF B-17s.

The result was a firestorm which engulfed the largely wooden centre of the city and consumed much of medieval Dresden and took perhaps 50,000 lives. Such was the destruction that even the meticulous accountancy that the German authorities excelled in after heavy raids could never arrive at an accurate casualty figure.

What is largely agreed is that the initial 5 Group raid was only moderately successful and the B-17s did little more than turn over the rubble and disturb what rescue work could be attempted. The real destructive might came with the raid in which Lancasters from North Lincolnshire figured very largely. The biggest proportion of the attacking force in that second wave was drawn from 1 Group.

The Lancasters carried mainly a mixture of 4,000lb blast bombs and incendiaries, the same mixture that had devastated Hamburg 18 months earlier and dozens of smaller German towns and cities. Given the right conditions, these loads could create fearful fire storms, and the right conditions existed in Dresden that night.

Dresden was one of four cities close to Germany's Eastern Front (the others were Berlin, Chemnitz and Leipzig) which were regarded as key centres to German resistance and through which reinforcements and supplies were passing for the front. That, at least was one view. Another was that Chemnitz and Dresden had largely been untouched by the bombing of the previous two years and their destruction was overdue. Yet another hypothesis put forward after the war is that the raid was intended as an illustration for the advancing Russians of just what the Allied air forces were capable of.

Certainly the raids, code-named Operation Thunderclap, enjoyed the patronage of Churchill although he managed to distance himself from them in later years. The Dresden raid achieved what it set out to do but the very necessity for the raid in the first place was to prove an embarrassment for Bomber Command and some of its leaders (but not Harris) after the war.

153. ***opposite page:*** *A happy reminder of Wickenby.*
154. ***left:*** *N-Nan of 626 Squadron at Wickenby in July 1945.*

Today it is possible to discern a certain unease when the subject is raised with some ex-Bomber Command crews. Many, it is true, still regard it as yet another trip (albeit a very long one) towards the completion of their tours. But all remember it, mostly because of what they witnessed that night.

It was possible to see the fires of Dresden a hundred, perhaps a hundred and fifty miles from the target. The bomber men knew the awesome power they were unleashing on that city. And most thought they knew why.

"I remember very clearly the briefing we had before the raid," said Geoff Robinson, a former flight engineer with 12 and 626 Squadrons at Wickenby. "We were told that the Russians had requested the raid because German troops were massing in the city in readiness for an attack on the Eastern Front. It was made quite clear to us that the raid was intended to help the Russians."

It was the same in briefing rooms across North Lincolnshire. 1 Group was striking a blow to help the Russian armies. It was a raid which could dramatically shorten the war.

"At the time I didn't know Dresden was one of the most historic cities in Germany," said Mr Robinson. "My geography did not extend to that."

Certainly the Wickenby records expressed no remorse at the damage done when they were completed the following day.

Dresden, the unknown compiler wrote, was a city "which had long awaited the inevitable Bomber Command attack." The raid was recorded as "first class, with many good fires raised."

The station had, in fact, supplied 31 aircraft for the second wave attack, 16 flying with the Pathfinders, and they reported a large area of the city on fire. The report added: "Many crews felt that this was one of the most spectacular attacks in which they had participated."

But it was Dresden, and the other raids like it, which some observers felt was the reason why no Bomber Command medal was struck after the war and why Air Marshal Harris did not receive the same kind of recognition as the leaders of the other armed forces. It was as though the country had forged a weapon and was then trying to distance itself from the effect that weapon had, choosing to ignore its own role in its creation and the satisfaction at its use when Britain had no other means of striking back at a Germany which dominated Europe from the North Cape to the Spanish border.

155. Transatlantic smiles from Jack Loughran and Jimmy Thompson, two Canadians serving with 625 Squadron.

The Bonds of Comradeship

EXTRAORDINARY BONDS were formed between the young men who nightly shared the perils of life and death over Germany.

For some those bonds have extended down the years, forging relationships which those who were not part of their experience can probably never begin to understand.

Take the case of the crew of Eddie Turner. He was a mid-upper gunner who, along with the six men he found himself crewed up with at a training unit, was posted to 100 Squadron at Waltham in 1944.

Thirty-seven operations later they finally parted at North Killingholme, one of the tour-expired crews with 550 Squadron, went on leave and found when they returned that they were being scattered to all parts of the RAF's empire.

Then 45 years later, they met again, reunited by those bonds forged in those long, dark nights over Germany.

Eddie Turner, for many years a policeman in North London, tells the story in his own words: "The RAF wartime photograph was taken at 550 Squadron during the winter of 1944. I had at times wondered if we would ever meet up again and now, 45 years afterwards, we have done, as the second photograph proves, five elderly gentlemen pictured in the same positions as they took up in the wartime photograph.

"In 1944 the five of us were part of a Lancaster bomber crew at North Killingholme. The rear gunner is missing from the photograph as he was playing cards in the sergeants' mess and didn't go down to the aircraft with the rest of us that morning. He emigrated to Australia after the war and is still there.

"Our flight engineer was in hospital, having fallen off his pedal cycle when we had almost completed our tour of operations. We finished our flying at North Killingholme with spare engineers and none of us have managed to trace our original engineer although we know he did originate from Somerset.

"So, back to 1944. We finished our 37 operations (11 on 100 Squadron and 26 with 550) and all went on leave expecting to meet up back at North Killingholme, but it was not to be. The war was still going on and I arrived back at the squadron to find the others had all been recalled after a few days, our pilot and wireless operator for flying duties, the navigator for flying control duties and the bomb-aimer for interviews and subsequent commission. I was later to end my days in the RAF in India and Singapore, finally coming home in 1947.

"About 20 years ago I did manage to trace our pilot who, like the rear gunner, had emigrated. Mike had left for Canada in the mid-Fifties and later went to America where he still lives. We met when I visited the USA but we lost contact again when Mike moved.

"The wireless operator and navigator I only contacted a matter of months ago, which leaves our bomb-aimer. We were in touch for a while some 30 years ago but again we lost contact and that meant he was the only problem when our navigator telephoned me to say Mike was coming over from America on holiday and would like us all to meet again.

"I still had an old telephone number for the bomb-aimer and all I could do was try . . . Ted answered the phone and so the second photograph came to life, as it were.

"For the record, we were and are: (back row, left to right) Edwin "Barney" Barnett, navigator, Eddie Turner, mid-upper gunner, Ted Evans, bomb-aimer; (front) Mike Smith, pilot, and Jack Moores, wireless operator.

"Barney lives near Rugby, Ted at Hemel Hempstead and Jack in Derby; Mike was awarded the DFC for his efforts in getting us to and from Germany. Life was to hold a twist for Mike as his son became a pilot in the US Air Force and flew in Vietnam; like father, like son — he returned safely."

As a "sprog" crew at Waltham, Eddie said that the 11 trips they did were accomplished in eight different Lancasters. "We were always given the ones that wouldn't fly very high!" he said. At North Killingholme they were allocated J-Jig only to be told no one had ever finished a tour in an aircraft with this code letter. But they did.

*156 & 157. **above:** Eddie Turner and crew*

A Rum Do

BACON AND eggs may have been the traditional pre-op meal but it was a tot of rum which most crews came home to. Sometimes, however, it could cause problems, as in the case of one 626 Squadron crew.

F/O A.H. Woods DFC and his crew were returning from their 18th op, a raid on Le Havre on September 8, 1944, when they were diverted to Faldingworth because a Lancaster on a training flight had crash-landed at Wickenby and closed the runway.

The pilot was the only rum drinker and took full advantage of the generosity of his crew and was just finishing his seventh tot when it was announced that Wickenby had re-opened and all 626 aircraft were to return.

The following is an extract from the excellent newsletter of the Wickenby Register, the 12 and 626 Squadrons association: "The flight engineer kept a close watch on him during start up and taxiing. He seemed all right. On the runway full power was applied and the aircraft proceeded down the runway in a straight line with the tail up at the right time. Well down the runway, the flight engineer looked across and saw the pilot in a daze, nodding off. He reached over, pulled back the stick and yelled for the bomb-aimer.

"The aircraft safely took to the air under the control of the bomb-aimer and the engineer, but the pilot had to be rapidly sobered up to get it down again. He was eventually made to drink the cold coffee dregs from all the flasks aboard and eventually made a better than normal touch-down at Wickenby!"

F/O Wood and crew went on to complete their tour with 626 and all are now members of the Wickenby Register.

A Word of Thanks

WHEN I began this project I had a handful of photographs, a few reference books and cuttings of three articles I had previously written on 1 Group airfields.

That I was able to amass more than 600 photographs from which to make a final selection and a small mountain of information on 1 Group, its airfields and squadrons is due in no small part to the men who served in those squadrons and on those airfields almost half a century ago. The response I had was overwhelming. My only regret is that space and time have not permitted me to include everything and contact all those who wrote to me.

I must make special mention of my old friend Peter Green, whose photograph and reference book library proved a wonderful starting point, and to Rowland Hardy, whose collections of 100 and 550 Squadron photographs made me realise that the task I had set myself was not impossible. With collections like that around, what else was there waiting to be discovered?

Special thanks must also go to that superb group of men (and women) who run the various squadron associations, whose help has been invaluable, people like Clem Koder and Eric Thale of the 625 Association, the enthusiastic band who run the Wickenby Register, Victor Redfearn, who entrusted me with what must be the priceless 101 Squadron photographic collection, Jim Wright, who runs the 166 Squadron Association, John Croft-Bednarski, one of the brave Poles who finished his war at Faldingworth, and Shirley Westrup, social secretary and a driving force behind the Elsham Wolds Association, which represents 103 and 576 Squadrons.

And then there were people like Squadron Leader Jimmy Bennett, a man able to fill many of the gaps in the official records, Mike Stedman, Herbert Harrison and the dozens of other former air and ground crew I spoke to and visited during the course of my research. Thank you one and all.

The story, however, may not be over yet. The publication of Part I of Maximum Effort led to such a response that I hope to write Part III for publication some time next year. If you can help with 1 Group memories, anecdotes and pictures, drop me a line at the Grimsby Evening Telegraph, 80 Cleethorpe Road, Grimsby DN31 3EH.

Patrick Otter

158. Aircrew and operations staff, B flight, 100 Squadron pictured at Waltham in 1944. The aircraft in the background are (from the left) Able-Mable, C-Charlie and E-Easy.